THE

5 IN 10

APPETIZER
COOKBOOK

Look for these other titles in the *5 in 10* series

The 5 in 10 Cookbook
Paula Hamilton

The 5 in 10 Chicken Breast Cookbook
Melanie Barnard and Brooke Dojny

The 5 in 10 Dessert Cookbook
Natalie Haughton

The 5 in 10 Pasta and Noodle Cookbook
Nancie McDermott

THE

5 IN 10

APPETIZER
COOKBOOK

5 Ingredients in
10 Minutes or Less

PAULA J. HAMILTON

A JOHN BOSWELL ASSOCIATES / KING HILL PRODUCTIONS BOOK

HEARST BOOKS

NEW YORK

This book is dedicated to
Edward, Julia and Jeffrey,
who make family dinners
so important.

Library of Congress Cataloging-in-Publication Data

Hamilton, Paula J.
    The 5 in 10 appetizer cookbook : 5 ingredients in 10 minutes
or less / [Paula J. Hamilton].
        p.   cm.
    "A John Boswell Associates/King Hill Productions book."
    Includes index.
    ISBN 0-688-13476-9
    1. Appetizers.   2. Quick and easy cookery.   I. Title.
II. Title: Five in ten appetizer cookbook.
TX740.H28   1994
641.8′12—dc20
                                                                        94-8505
                                                                        CIP

Printed in the United States of America

First Edition

1   2   3   4   5   6   7   8   9   10

Book design by Barbara Cohen Aronica

CONTENTS

4. ELEGANT BUT EASY 69

Luxurious ingredients and showstopping presentation distinguish these special 5 in 10 appetizers and first courses: Sweet Corn and Shrimp Cakes, Salmon Fillet with Red Pepper Coulis and Avocado Pancakes with Crabmeat.

5. MARVELOUS AND MEATLESS 94

These contemporary taste tempters range from Straw Potato Pancakes, made with white and sweet potatoes, and Asparagus Spears with Sesame Mayonnaise to Mozzarella Cheese Chunks with Marinara Sauce and Pesto-stuffed Mushrooms.

6. HOT AND SPICY 114

Those who like it hot will like it here: Jerked Chicken with Papaya, Santa Fe Fondue, Chili Cheddar Wafers and Creole Shrimp are just a few of the fiery appetizers featured.

7. FROM THE GRILL 133

Whether you're doing your grilling on an outdoor barbecue or under your oven broilers, you'll welcome easy entertaining ideas like Chicken Satay, Garlicky Pork Kebabs, Grilled Ratatouille and Swordfish Brochettes with Mango Lime Sauce.

8. Salads and Other Cool First Courses 155

Stay calm, cool and collected with in-a-flash starters and side dishes such as Chinese Sesame Noodles, Corn Salad with Basil and Tomatoes, Radishes and Red Onion Salad and Tuna with White Beans and Tapenade.

INTRODUCTION

Appetizers that taste as good as they look don't have to be complicated. In *The 5 in 10 Appetizer Cookbook* you'll find over 165 recipes, ranging from delicious dips and fancy finger food to unusual first-course salads. All of the recipes can be prepared in 10 minutes or less using just 5 ingredients—not counting salt and pepper.

Appetizer parties fit in perfectly with today's busy lifestyles because they are fun and easy to put on, and the food can be as eclectic as the conversation. In fact, appetizers, loosely defined as small bites, encourage adventurous eating.

Although traditionally they have been served as a teaser before a meal, appetizers can easily become an informal meal by themselves. They can be served hot or cold, in bite-size pieces or family-style on large platters. For parties, you have a choice of combining a variety of these quick dishes together on an appetizer buffet or stretching out the surprise by presenting them one at a time. Guests love not knowing what will come out of your kitchen next.

Another advantage is that appetizers lend themselves to impromptu entertaining. So don't worry if people drop in unexpectedly. By keeping a well-stocked larder filled with high-quality convenience foods, such as spicy salsas, canned beans, roasted sweet red peppers, quick-cooking polenta, marinated artichoke hearts, tangy olives, sun-dried tomatoes and pesto, you can whip up recipes like a zesty Warm Chile Bean Dip, savory Toasted Olive Canapés or Roasted Red Pepper Dip in no time.

Produce markets, supermarkets and delis are also helping hurried hosts by selling ready-to-use items, such as trimmed and rinsed spinach, peeled and cut fresh pineapple, freshly grated cheese and baked pizza breads to use as a base for your own instant pizza. By keeping some of these prepared foods on hand, the menu can expand should the guest list suddenly grow. Also remember, you don't have to make everything yourself. A little sleight of hand goes a long way. It only takes a few minutes, some store-bought pesto and a handful of pine nuts, for example, to turn a wheel of plain Brie into a fancy Brie Torte. A slice of savory pâté from the local charcuterie or deli can be personalized by being sliced and served with a homemade spicy orange mustard sauce alongside. No one has to know that you whipped it up in less than five minutes.

Because these recipes rely on only a few ingredients, it's important that each one be as flavorful as possible. That's why I recommend buying fresh produce in season. In general, when the price is the best, so is the flavor. A first-course salad made in winter with pale, mealy, bland tomatoes has nothing in common with one prepared in season with perfect, sweet, juicy, vine-ripened tomatoes. Pick and choose your recipes with an eye to availability and quality of ingredients.

When planning appetizer party menus, strive for variety and balance. For example, serve both hot and cold appetizers that vary in color, texture and flavor. As a general rule of thumb, plan about four appetizer bites per person before a dinner and about 12 per person during a cocktail party that goes on for several hours. I've tried to make this easy for you by giving the number of pieces a recipe makes wherever it was practical.

To save time and to get yourself out of the kitchen, balance hot hors d'oeuvres that must be cooked or reheated at the last moment with plenty of spiced nuts, seasoned olives and something like the quickly assembled Smoked Salmon and Herb Terrine that can be made in advance.

Here are some other timesaving tips: Get organized before you start any recipe. Read it carefully, then assemble all of the ingredients and equipment that are needed. When making canapés or finger food in quantity, it often saves time to set up an assembly line. Be sure to keep your knives sharp. Not only will you find it easier and faster to slice, you'll also be less likely to cut yourself. Parchment paper is a great timesaver. Use it to line your baking pans to prevent sticking and to cut down on cleanup. A wide pastry brush is helpful for basting grilled kebabs and glazing broiled appetizers. And if you make a lot of appetizer kebabs, you may want to invest in some short metal skewers to eliminate having to presoak the bamboo ones.

The recipes in this collection include dips and spreads, canapés, baked savories, first-course salads, grilled kebabs and several dozen ideas for unusual pick-up appetizers. They were all created with one goal: to be doable enough to let you be a guest at your own party, which is easy with the 5 in 10 principle.

1 DAZZLING DIPS AND SUPERB SPREADS

Everyone loves dips and spreads. It's impossible to resist a light Smoked Trout Mousse or a spicy black bean puree topped with small cubes of velvety, pale green avocado.

Hurried hosts and hostesses are wise to have a variety of dip and spread recipes in their repertoire. With a food processor and a few flavorful ingredients, many of which are pantry staples, it's possible to whip up a selection of savory spreadables in mere minutes. These can also be put together in advance and stored, covered, in the refrigerator.

The recipes in this chapter illustrate just how varied these easy appetizers can be. For example, there are hot and cold bean dips, a creamy blue cheese spread studded with toasted hazelnuts, a piquant red pepper dip flavored with garlic and capers, a shrimp cocktail spread and a Greek Potato and Garlic Dip.

While most of us grew up with potato chips and dips, raw or lightly cooked vegetables, thin wedges of apple or pear, pita triangles and, of course, corn tortilla chips are now the order of the day. Here's a great chance to be creative with your presentation. Brightly colored vegetables can be piled up in baskets with a bowl of dip tucked in at the side or arranged in a circle on a large platter, with the dip in the center.

BLACK BEAN AND AVOCADO DIP

Creamy chunks of pale green avocado contrast nicely with spicy pureed black beans in this delicious dip. Crisp yellow corn tortilla chips are perfect dippers.

1 can (15 ounces) black beans
1 garlic clove
½ cup thick and chunky medium-hot prepared red salsa
½ teaspoon ground cumin
1 small ripe avocado

1. Drain the black beans and place them in the bowl of a food processor or blender. Pulse several times.

2. Crush the garlic through a press into the processor. Add the salsa and cumin and continue processing until smooth. Spoon the black bean mixture into a shallow serving dish.

3. Just before serving, cut the avocado in half and remove the pit. Peel the avocado, then cut it into ³/₈-inch dice. Sprinkle the diced avocado on top of the bean dip.

MAKES 2 CUPS

LEMONY CHICK-PEA PUREE

There are dozens of variations of hummus or pureed seasoned chick-peas. Sometimes the mixture is seasoned with tahini or sesame seed paste. Often ground cumin is added. In this version, sesame chili oil imparts a slight Asian flavor and a sprinkling of chili powder on top contributes some spice. Serve it with a basket of warm pita breads.

1 can (15½ ounces) chick-peas (also called garbanzo beans)
1 large garlic clove
2 tablespoons lemon juice
¼ teaspoon sesame chili oil
    Dash of salt
½ teaspoon chili powder

1. Drain the chick-peas, reserving the liquid. Mince the garlic in the food processor. Add the chick-peas and pulse several times. Then add the lemon juice, sesame chili oil and salt. Continue processing, adding 1 to 2 tablespoons of the reserved liquid, if necessary, until the mixture is smooth.

2. Taste for seasoning, adding more chili oil or salt if needed. Spoon the puree into a serving bowl and sprinkle chili powder over the top.

MAKES 2 CUPS

WARM CHILE BEAN DIP

Serve glasses of iced beer with this warm bean dip. If you like heat, add some hot jalapeño peppers or salsa. You can also add bits of leftover chicken or pork. The variations are endless. Serve with crisp tortilla chips.

1 can (16 ounces) vegetarian refried beans
1 can (4 ounces) diced green chiles
1 small tomato
½ cup sliced ripe olives
1 cup shredded sharp Cheddar cheese

1. Spoon the beans into a shallow microwave-safe 1-quart casserole, smoothing the top. Sprinkle the green chiles over the refried beans. Dice the tomato and sprinkle it over the chiles. Then sprinkle on the olives.

2. Cover with vented microwave-safe plastic wrap and microwave on High for 3 minutes. Sprinkle on the cheese, cover again and microwave about 3 minutes longer, until the cheese melts.

MAKES ABOUT 3 CUPS

GARLICKY WHITE BEAN DIP

Thanks to the convenience of canned beans and creamy garlic herb cheese spread, this flavorful dip is ready in no time. Serve with crisp vegetable sticks for dipping. Carrots, jicama, celery and colorful red, green and yellow bell peppers are good choices.

1 can (15 ounces) white beans
1 package (4 ounces) garlic herb cheese spread, such as
   Boursin or Alouette
½ teaspoon salt
¼ teaspoon hot pepper sauce
2 teaspoons minced fresh chives

1. Place the undrained beans in the container of a food processor or blender along with the garlic herb cheese spread, salt and hot pepper sauce. Process until the mixture is smooth.

2. Spoon the bean dip into a serving bowl and sprinkle the chives on top.

MAKES 2 CUPS

HONEY HAM AND
WHITE BEAN SPREAD

Using pureed canned white beans as the base for dips and spreads, instead of cream cheese, sour cream or mayonnaise, trades in unnecessary fat for good nutrition. Baked smoked ham, honey mustard, hot pepper sauce and chives add lively flavor to this spread. It's delicious slathered on crisp onion crackers or as a dip for crudités.

$\frac{1}{2}$ pound baked smoked ham
1 can (15 ounces) white beans
$1\frac{1}{2}$ tablespoons honey mustard
$\frac{1}{4}$ teaspoon hot pepper sauce, or more to taste
2 tablespoons minced fresh chives

1. Cut the ham in small pieces and place in a food processor. Pulse several times to chop coarsely.

2. Rinse the beans and drain. Add them to the ham along with the mustard and process until the mixture is smooth. Season with the hot sauce.

3. Spoon the spread into a serving bowl and sprinkle the chives over the top.

MAKES 2 CUPS

SIMPLY GREAT GUACAMOLE

Tart tomatillos, the major ingredient in salsa verde, have a wonderful influence on avocados. They make the fruit taste sweeter and nuttier. This all-purpose avocado dip is a delicious spread for canapés, especially when topped with thinly sliced tomatoes and radishes, It's also a great sandwich filling and terrific scooped up on lightly salted tortilla chips. I prefer guacamole to have a slightly chunky texture. If you want yours to be smoother, combine all of the ingredients in a food processor.

1 large ripe avocado (about 10 ounces)
3 tablespoons bottled salsa verde
2 tablespoons minced onion
1 tablespoon chopped fresh cilantro
1 tablespoon lemon juice
1/4 teaspoon salt

1. Cut the avocado in half and twist the halves to separate them. Remove the pit, then scoop out the avocado and place it in a medium bowl. Mash the avocado with a fork.

2. Add the salsa verde, minced onion, chopped cilantro, lemon juice and salt. Stir until it's as smooth as you like. Serve immediately.

MAKES ABOUT 1 1/2 CUPS

MUSHROOM PÂTÉ

Spread this tasty mushroom pâté on crisp sesame crackers or on croutons cut out of toasted white bread.

$1/2$ pound mushrooms
$1^1/2$ teaspoons bottled chopped garlic in oil
1 tablespoon finely chopped fresh tarragon or $1/2$ teaspoon dried
1 tablespoon tomato paste
$1/8$ teaspoon cayenne pepper

1. Wipe the mushrooms and place them in a food processor. Pulse several times, then process about 1 minute until the mushrooms are very finely chopped.

2. Place the garlic with its oil in a medium frying pan. Add the mushrooms and cook over high heat, stirring frequently, until the mixture is nearly dry, about 6 minutes. Stir in the tarragon, tomato paste and cayenne pepper, blending well. Serve this pâté warm or at room temperature.

MAKES $3/4$ CUP

BLACK OLIVE TAPENADE

I like to keep this versatile olive paste on hand to add zesty flavor to canapés, pizzas, seafood and vegetable salads. You can substitute ripe olives for the Kalamata olives, but the flavor won't be as interesting. Even though Kalamata olives come already pitted, it's always a good idea to check. Every so often an olive pit sneaks into the jar.

1 large garlic clove
1 jar (about 8 ounces) pitted Kalamata olives (about 1 cup)
$1/4$ cup extra virgin olive oil
3 flat anchovy fillets
1 tablespoon brandy

1. Place the garlic clove in the food processor and pulse several times. Rinse the olives, then add them to the garlic and process about 30 seconds.

2. Scrape down the sides of the bowl. Add 3 tablespoons of the olive oil, the anchovies and the brandy and process until the tapenade is smooth, about 2 minutes. Use immediately or spoon it into a jar and pour the remaining olive oil on top. This will keep for weeks in the refrigerator.

MAKES ABOUT 1 CUP

ROASTED RED PEPPER DIP

Wonderful with chips, pita triangles or crudités, this tangy dip can be diluted with a little pasta cooking water and used as a sauce.

2 large garlic cloves
1 jar (12 ounces) roasted red bell peppers
2 tablespoons extra virgin olive oil
$1/2$ teaspoon salt
$1/4$ teaspoon cayenne pepper
    Freshly ground black pepper
$1^1/2$ tablespoons tiny (nonpareil) capers, including some of the brine in which they're packed

1. Place the garlic cloves in a food processor. Pulse several times to chop; scrape down the sides of the bowl. Add the roasted red peppers, olive oil, salt, cayenne and black pepper. Process until the mixture is smooth.

2. Add the capers and process 30 seconds longer to combine.

MAKES 1$1/2$ CUPS

GREEK POTATO AND GARLIC DIP

This is the Greek national dip, *skordalia*. It is sometimes made with bread or nuts, but this potato version is the most popular. Normally, a cook would have to allow at least 20 minutes to boil the potatoes, but frozen mashed potatoes make this recipe in record time. Serve with slices of zucchini, sticks of celery or fennel or baguette slices.

1/4 cup extra virgin olive oil
3 to 4 garlic cloves, crushed through a press
3 cups (14 ounces) frozen mashed potatoes
2 tablespoons fresh lemon juice
1/4 teaspoon salt
1/4 teaspoon freshly ground pepper

1. In a medium saucepan, heat the olive oil over low heat. Add the garlic and cook, stirring, until it begins to turn gold, 1 to 2 minutes.

2. Immediately pour in 1 1/2 cups water and bring to a boil. Stir in the frozen mashed potatoes and bring to a simmer. Cook, stirring often, until thickened, about 4 minutes. Stir in the lemon juice, salt and pepper. Serve warm or at room temperature.

MAKES 3 CUPS

SUN-DRIED TOMATO PESTO

The rich sunny flavors of the Mediterranean are captured in this versatile sun-dried tomato pesto. Spread a thin layer of the vivid spread on crostini, appetizer pizzas or rounds of grilled polenta. Fold a spoonful into mayonnaise or vinaigrette for appetizer salads or a dipping sauce for grilled kebabs or toss a small amount into hot pasta for a savory first course. Stored covered in a glass jar, it will keep for several weeks in the refrigerator.

1 large garlic clove
3 wide flat strips of orange zest (each about 3 inches long)
1 jar (8 ounces) sun-dried tomatoes preserved in olive oil
1/4 cup grated Parmesan cheese
1/2 teaspoon dried thyme leaves

1. Place the garlic clove and orange zest in a food processor and process until finely chopped, about 1 minute.

2. Add the tomatoes and the oil in which they are packed, the cheese and the thyme, and process until the mixture is well combined but still slightly chunky, 2 to 3 minutes.

MAKES 1 1/4 CUPS

SAUCE VERTE

This zesty dip comes out slightly different depending on what green herbs and vegetables are available. Although I always start with a shallot and end with mayonnaise and vinegar, I vary the other ingredients, sometimes using parsley, green onions and other fresh herbs in addition to or in place of the ingredients given here. This spread or dip is especially delicious with cubes of ham, smoked chicken and other cured or smoked meats and fish.

1 large shallot
1 bunch of watercress
1 bunch of chives
1 tablespoon tarragon-flavored vinegar plus 2 teaspoons tarragon leaves (from the vinegar)
³/₄ cup mayonnaise

1. Place the shallot in a food processor and pulse several times to chop. Rinse and dry the watercress. Discard the thicker stems and place the rest in the food processor. Rinse and dry the chives and cut them into 2-inch lengths. Add the chives and tarragon leaves to the food processor. Pulse several times, until everything is coarsely chopped.

2. Add the mayonnaise and vinegar and continue to process about 2 minutes longer, until the sauce is fairly smooth.

MAKES ABOUT 1 ¹/₂ CUPS

CREAMY BLUE CHEESE SPREAD

You could thin this spread out with a few tablespoons of milk and serve it as a dip for fresh fruit. Toasted chopped hazelnuts are a nice garnish.

1 package (8 ounces) cream cheese
1 package (4 ounces) blue cheese
2 tablespoons Cognac or brandy
1 teaspoon dried tarragon
½ cup hazelnuts

1. Place the cream cheese, blue cheese, Cognac and tarragon in a food processor and process until smooth and creamy, about 2 minutes.

2. Coarsely chop the hazelnuts and place them in a skillet. Toast over moderately high heat, stirring frequently, until they turn golden and smell nutty, about 3 to 4 minutes.

3. Stir ⅓ cup of the hazelnuts into the spread. Spoon the mixture into a serving bowl and sprinkle the remaining nuts over the cheese.

MAKES ABOUT 1 ½ CUPS

BRIE TORTE

Here's a quick way to dress up a large wheel of Brie for a party. You can also use pesto made with basil or cilantro or even tapenade (olive paste). If you have a few nasturtiums or other edible flowers, use them to garnish the serving platter. Serve crackers or thin slices of toasted country-style bread with the cheese.

1 wheel (2.2 pounds) Brie cheese
1 1/2 cups sun-dried tomato pesto
2/3 cup pine nuts or slivered almonds

1. With a long, sharp knife, cut the wedge of Brie in half horizontally and separate the two halves. Spread half of the pesto on top of the bottom half of cheese. Cover with the other wedge of cheese.

2. Spread the remaining pesto on top and sprinkle on the pine nuts, pressing them in slightly.

20 TO 24 SERVINGS

NOTE: For a small gathering of 6 or so, this same recipe can be made with an 8-ounce wheel of Brie, 1/3 cup tomato pesto and 1/4 cup pine nuts.

BAKED CAMEMBERT WITH A SWEET PECAN CRUST

Crisp slices of tart green apples are the perfect base on which to spread melted Camembert and toasted pecans. When choosing Camembert, look for plump, slightly soft rounds of cheese with a golden-tinged rind. Avoid any with dry, hardened edges, an indication that the cheese may be overripe.

1/2 pound round or wedge of Camembert cheese
3 tablespoons dark brown sugar
1 tablespoon white wine or apple juice
1/3 cup pecan halves
2 to 3 tart apples

1. Preheat the oven to 475 degrees F. Place the cheese in a shallow ovenproof dish that's suitable for serving.

2. In a small bowl, stir together the brown sugar and the wine to make a paste and spread over the top of the cheese. Cover with the pecan halves, pressing them in slightly.

3. Place the cheese in the oven and bake 8 minutes, or until the cheese begins to melt and the pecans are toasted. If the cheese begins to melt before the nuts are nicely browned, broil 1 to 2 minutes before serving.

4. While the cheese is baking, rinse the apples. Core, then cut them into thin wedges. Serve the apple slices alongside the hot cheese.

6 SERVINGS

GARLIC-HERB CHEESE SPREAD

Cream cheese and butter whip into the most sensuous spread, especially when flavored with garlic, green onions and herbes de Provence. You could also create your own house specialty by adding other herbs such as dill, chives, garlic chives or lemon thyme. Serve as a spread for crackers, canapés, sandwiches or as a dip with fresh vegetables.

3 green onions
2 garlic cloves
1 package (8 ounces) cream cheese
1 stick ($\frac{1}{2}$ cup) butter
1$\frac{1}{2}$ teaspoons herbes de Provence

1. Trim the green onions and cut them into 1-inch lengths. Place them in a food processor. Add the garlic and pulse several times until coarsely chopped.

2. Add the cream cheese, butter and herbes de Provence. Process until the spread is smooth and creamy.

MAKES ABOUT 1$\frac{2}{3}$ CUPS

PESTO YOGURT CHEESE

Another versatile spread that can be served with crudités or baguette slices. Yogurt can sometimes be a little too thin to be an efficient dip, but draining off some of the whey firms it up nicely to a cheeselike consistency. Don't try this with nonfat cheese—it's too thin to have the whey pressed out.

2 cups plain low-fat yogurt
1/3 cup prepared pesto
2 tablespoons pine nuts

1. Line a wire sieve with a double thickness of rinsed, squeezed-out cheesecloth. Place the yogurt in the sieve, and bring up the loose ends of the cheesecloth. Place a saucer or plate that fits the sieve on top of the yogurt. Press firmly on the saucer to extract about 1/2 cup of whey from the yogurt. (This will take 3 or 4 minutes.) Transfer the yogurt to a medium bowl and stir in the pesto.

2. In a small nonstick skillet, cook the pine nuts over medium heat, stirring often, until lightly browned. Let cool for a couple of minutes, then chop coarsely.

3. Transfer the dip to a serving bowl and sprinkle with the pine nuts.

MAKES 1 3/4 CUPS

PORT WINE CHEESE SPREAD

Surround a crock of this creamy Cheddar cheese spread with apples, pears, grapes, celery sticks and assorted crackers. You can prepare this spread ahead and keep it covered in the refrigerator, but it's best to serve it at room temperature.

1 package (8 ounces) shredded sharp Cheddar cheese
1 package (8 ounces) cream cheese
$1/4$ cup ruby port wine
$1/2$ cup chopped walnuts

1. Place the Cheddar and cream cheese in a microwave-safe bowl and microwave on High for about 45 seconds to soften.

2. Add the port and stir vigorously until the mixture is smooth. Fold in the walnuts and spoon the mixture into a crock or serving bowl. Serve at room temperature.

MAKES ABOUT $2^2/3$ CUPS

FRUITED CURRY DIP

This versatile dip goes well with crunchy vegetables, grilled chicken and shellfish or fresh fruit.

1 cup sour cream
2 tablespoons mango chutney
2 tablespoons orange juice
1 teaspoon Dijon mustard
1 teaspoon curry powder

1. Place the sour cream in a small bowl. Stir in the mango chutney, orange juice, mustard and curry powder, blending well.

2. Spoon the dip into a bowl, cover and refrigerate until serving time.

MAKES 1 ¼ CUPS

TUSCAN CHICKEN LIVER SPREAD

Spread this savory but sweet meld of chicken livers, slivers of sun-dried tomatoes and capers on slices of fresh country-style bread, melba toast or small pita breads.

$^1/_3$ cup slivered sun-dried tomatoes packed in oil plus 1
   tablespoon of the oil
1 pound chicken livers
3 tablespoons port wine
2 tablespoons tiny (nonpareil) capers plus 1 tablespoon of the
   packing brine
$^1/_4$ teaspoon salt
$^1/_4$ teaspoon freshly ground pepper

1. Heat the oil from the tomatoes in a large frying pan over high heat. Add the chicken livers and cook over medium-high heat, stirring occasionally, until the livers are brown outside and pink inside, 3 to 5 minutes.

2. Place the livers in a food processor. Add the port to the frying pan and bring to a boil, scraping up any browned bits from the bottom of the pan with a wooden spoon. Pour this liquid over the livers in the food processor and puree until smooth.

3. Stir in the slivered tomatoes and capers plus the liquid from the capers. Add the salt and pepper. Spoon the spread into a crock to serve.

MAKES ABOUT 1 $^1/_4$ CUPS

SMOKED SALMON SPREAD

Save money by buying lox trimmings, rather than perfect slices, for this recipe. Serve as an appetizer spread for miniature bagels or cocktail rye or use as a filling in rolled appetizer omelets.

⅓ pound smoked salmon trimmings
1 lemon
½ small onion
1 package (8 ounces) cream cheese
2 tablespoons minced fresh dill

1. Place the smoked salmon in a food processor and pulse a few times. You don't want the fish to be chopped too finely. Remove the salmon to a bowl.

2. Using a coarse grater or zester, remove the outermost colored part, the zest, of the lemon. Juice half of the lemon (about 2 tablespoons).

3. Cut up the onion and place in a food processor; pulse several times to chop. Add the cream cheese, lemon zest and juice and dill and process about 1 minute, until mixture is well blended. Fold the cream cheese into the smoked salmon.

MAKES ABOUT 2 CUPS

WARM SCALLOP DIP

Serve this fabulous, rich, velvety-textured dip with plenty of thinly sliced French bread or on crisp crostini (thin toast). You can also bake it in tiny toast cups or prepared tart shells. This dip is best served hot. If it cools down, just return it to the broiler again to heat through.

$^{1}\!/_{2}$ pound scallops
$^{1}\!/_{2}$ cup shredded Jarlsberg cheese (2 ounces)
$^{1}\!/_{2}$ cup mayonnaise
1 teaspoon bottled chopped garlic in oil
Grated zest of 1 lemon ($^{3}\!/_{4}$ teaspoon)

1. Preheat the broiler. Coarsely chop the scallops. In a medium bowl, combine the scallops, cheese, mayonnaise, garlic and lemon zest, blending well.

2. Spread the mixture in a gratin or other shallow pan, making sure that it is no more than $^{1}\!/_{2}$ inch thick to ensure even cooking.

3. Broil 3 to 4 inches from the source of heat for about 5 minutes, until the scallops are cooked through and the dip is golden brown and bubbling. Serve at once.

4 TO 6 SERVINGS

SHRIMP COCKTAIL SPREAD

Everybody loves shrimp cocktail, but it can be pricey to serve to a crowd. Here, it is transformed into a spread to be served on crackers, a deliciously frugal way to satisfy the shellfish lovers at a party, and there are always plenty of those! If you wish, for color, place the cream cheese on a bed of large romaine lettuce leaves or kale.

3/4 cup red cocktail sauce
1 celery rib, finely chopped
1 package (8 ounces) cream cheese
6 ounces cooked bay shrimp
  Sesame-topped crackers, for serving

1. In a medium bowl, combine the cocktail sauce and celery.

2. Place the cream cheese on a serving platter. Pour the sauce over the cheese, then top with the shrimp, letting the shrimp cascade down the sides. Serve immediately with a knife, letting each guest spread the cheese with a bit of sauce and shrimp onto the crackers.

6 TO 8 SERVINGS

SMOKED TROUT MOUSSE

It's hard to stop eating this creamy smoked trout spread. Serve it with crackers, wedges of warm pita, thinly sliced pumpernickel or rye bread or with crudités.

2 boneless smoked trout (about 6 ounces each)
1 package (8 ounces) cream cheese, softened
1 cup sour cream
$\frac{1}{2}$ cup marinated, slivered sun-dried tomatoes
1 teaspoon dried thyme leaves

1. Remove the skin from the trout and place the trout fillets in a food processor. Pulse several times to chop coarsely.

2. Add the cream cheese, sour cream, sun-dried tomatoes and thyme and puree until smooth, about 2 minutes. Pour into a bowl and serve. Or cover and refrigerate to serve later.

MAKES ABOUT 3 $\frac{1}{2}$ CUPS

2 Fabulous
Finger Food

This finger food includes everything from bite-size pastry cups filled with salsa-flavored chicken to small squares of frittata studded with smoked salami and broccoli. Some examples, such as Baby Shrimp in Endive or Zucchini Rounds with Ham Mousse, are served cold. Other possibilities—Deviled Chicken Nuggets and Shiitake Mushroom Fritters, for example—are best served hot. At the liveliest parties, it's nice to have a mix of both.

Some recipes in this chapter are designed to be served as individual portions. Others, such as the Zesty Olives and Spiced Almonds, can be just put into bowls and passed or set on a side table or buffet. Some are best on toothpicks.

Although you won't need plates for the appetizers in this chapter, do provide plenty of napkins. Cloth cocktail napkins are, of course, charming. Sometimes you can pick them up inexpensively in antique stores and at auctions. And these days there is a huge range of decorative and playful paper cocktail napkins available in supermarkets and at gift and party shops.

SPICY CORN MUFFINS

Bits of smoky ham and spicy jalapeño peppers lend a Southwestern flavor to these miniature corn muffins.

2 fresh jalapeño peppers
1/2 pound Black Forest ham
2 eggs
2/3 cup milk
2 boxes (81/2 ounces each) corn muffin mix

1. Preheat the oven to 425 degrees F. Seed and finely mince the jalapeño peppers. Cut the ham into 1/4-inch dice.

2. Place the eggs and milk in a medium bowl and whisk until blended. Add the corn muffin mix, minced jalapeño pepper, and diced ham. Stir just until the dry ingredients are moistened.

3. Fill 48 greased mini-muffin cups almost to the top with the corn muffin batter. Bake for 8 minutes, or until the muffins are golden brown.

MAKES 48

CURRIED CHICKEN BISCUITS

Fill hot flaky biscuits with curried chicken salad for a hearty appetizer. If you like, you could also add ¼ cup of Major Grey's chutney to the chicken mixture.

2 tubes (10 ounces each) refrigerated flaky biscuits with butter flavor
¾ cup sliced almonds
¾ pound cooked chicken
⅔ cup mayonnaise
2 teaspoons curry powder
¼ teaspoon salt
¼ teaspoon freshly ground black pepper

1. Preheat the oven to 425 degrees F. Place the biscuits on an ungreased baking sheet and bake about 8 minutes, until golden brown.

2. Meanwhile, toast the almonds in a dry frying pan over medium heat, stirring occasionally, until golden brown, 3 to 4 minutes. Transfer them to a small bowl and set aside.

3. Cut the chicken into ⅜-inch dice. In a medium bowl, blend together the mayonnaise, curry powder, salt and pepper. Add the chicken and mix well. Fold in the toasted almonds.

4. When the biscuits are done, remove them from the oven. Split them in half and fill each one with 1 rounded tablespoon of the curried chicken.

MAKES 20

FLAKY BISCUITS WITH BAKED HAM AND HERBED HONEY BUTTER

Spread soft honey butter on warm biscuits and tuck in thinly sliced Black Forest ham for an easy appetizer that everyone loves. You can also use hot sweet mustard for a slightly zestier spread.

2 tubes (10 ounces each) refrigerated flaky biscuits
1 stick unsalted butter
1½ tablespoons honey mustard
1 teaspoon dried thyme leaves
¾ pound thinly sliced Black Forest ham

1. Preheat the oven to 425 degrees F. Place the biscuits on an ungreased baking sheet and bake about 8 minutes, until they are golden brown.

2. While the biscuits are baking, prepare the honey butter. Place the butter in a small glass bowl. If it is hard, heat it in the microwave on High for about 10 seconds to soften. Add the honey mustard and blend well. Stir in the thyme.

3. When the biscuits are done, remove them from the oven. Split each biscuit in half and spread with about ½ tablespoon of the honey butter. Tuck in a slice of ham and serve while still warm.

MAKES 20

DOLMAS WITH MINTED YOGURT SAUCE

Now that delicious dolmas (stuffed grape leaves) are available already prepared in tins and at delis, I rarely bother making them from scratch. All that's necessary is to arrange them attractively on a platter and stir up a garlic- and mint-scented yogurt sauce to serve alongside. "*Kali orexi*," or good eating, as they say in Greece.

1 can (13 ounces) prepared dolmas (about 15)
1 large garlic clove
1 lemon
2 tablespoons chopped fresh mint
⅔ cup nonfat plain yogurt

1. Arrange the dolmas on a serving platter. Mince the garlic. Grate the zest from the lemon and then juice the lemon.

2. Stir the garlic, lemon zest and chopped mint into the yogurt. Taste for tartness, gradually adding the lemon juice, if it is needed.

3 OR 4 SERVINGS

SHIITAKE MUSHROOM FRITTERS

Although you could use cultivated mushrooms, shiitake or other wild mushrooms provide a wonderful earthy flavor. Serve them as is or with lemon aioli (mayonnaise flavored with lemon juice and minced garlic). For an elegant first course, scatter the mushrooms over a salad of baby lettuces dressed with a lemon vinaigrette.

1 cup cornbread stuffing mix
1 tablespoon herbes de Provence
2 eggs
½ pound medium fresh shiitake mushrooms
2 cups vegetable oil

1. Whirl the stuffing mix in a food processor for a few seconds until the crumbs are fine. Pour into a shallow bowl and stir in the herbes de Provence.

2. Crack the eggs into a bowl and whip with a fork. Cut the stems from the mushrooms and discard. Rinse the mushroom caps and pat dry.

3. Heat the oil in a deep frying pan until it reaches 375 degrees F. Meanwhile, dip the mushroom caps in the eggs, then in the crumbs, turning to coat both sides. Fry the coated mushrooms in several batches without crowding until they are brown and crispy, 2½ to 3 minutes per batch. Remove with a slotted spoon and drain on paper towels. Serve hot.

6 SERVINGS

ZESTY OLIVES

Olives, lemon and garlic are a fabulous culinary trio. While these are wonderful as soon as they are made, they can certainly be refrigerated for a week or two, where they will continue to marinate and mellow in flavor. Just about any Mediterranean olive variety, black or green, works. I've used Kalamata, Nyons and Sicilian green, all successfully. Do not use canned California ripe black olives in this recipe.

$\frac{1}{2}$ pound Mediterranean olives
$\frac{1}{2}$ teaspoon Italian herb seasoning
$\frac{1}{4}$ teaspoon crushed hot red pepper
1 garlic clove
1 lemon

1. In a small bowl, place the olives, herbs and hot pepper. Crush the garlic through a press into the bowl.

2. Using a zester or hand-held cheese grater, remove the outermost colored peel, or zest, from the lemon and add to the olives. Squeeze the juice from half of the lemon over the olives and toss well.

8 SERVINGS

SPICED ALMONDS

Olive oil imparts a wonderful flavor to toasted almonds. The secret to this favorite tapas is heating the nuts and oil together. Sprinkle with a combination of chili powder, ground cumin and garlic salt before serving.

1 pound blanched whole raw almonds
2 tablespoons olive oil
1½ teaspoons chili powder
1 teaspoon ground cumin
½ teaspoon seasoned salt

1. Place the almonds and oil in a large frying pan. Cook over medium-high heat, stirring often, until the almonds are a light golden brown, about 6 minutes.

2. Sprinkle the chili powder, cumin and salt over the nuts and continue to cook, stirring, 1 minute longer. Transfer to a bowl and let cool slightly or to room temperature before serving.

MAKES ABOUT 3⅓ CUPS

COCONUT CHICKEN BITES

Moist chicken coated with crispy, slightly sweet coconut makes a delicious appetizer. To be extra festive, serve some mango chutney seasoned with curry alongside as a dipping sauce.

2 cups vegetable oil
1 whole skinless, boneless chicken breast (about 10 ounces)
1 package (7 ounces) flaked coconut
2/3 cup beer
1/2 cup flour

1. Pour the oil into a deep frying pan and heat over high heat to 375 degrees F. To test the temperature of the oil, drop in a shred of coconut; if it sizzles immediately, the oil is hot enough.

2. Meanwhile, cut the chicken into 1-inch squares. Place the coconut on a plate. Pour the beer into a bowl. Add the flour and whisk until smooth. Dip the chicken pieces in the beer batter, then roll in the coconut to coat all sides.

3. Add the chicken squares to the oil in 2 or 3 batches, being careful not to crowd them. Cook, turning occasionally, until golden brown and cooked through, about 2 minutes. Remove the chicken with a slotted spoon and drain on paper towels. Serve hot.

6 SERVINGS

CHICKEN SALSA CUPS

Refrigerated won ton wrappers are a great convenience. With them you can make crisp, bite-size pastry cups in 6 minutes. If you like your food fiery, use a hot salsa or add a light sprinkling or crushed hot red pepper to this recipe.

12 won ton wrappers (about 3 inches square)
1 whole skinless, boneless chicken breast (about 10 ounces)
1½ tablespoons olive oil
½ cup thick and chunky red salsa
12 sprigs of cilantro

1. Preheat the oven to 400 degrees F. Place the won ton wrappers in miniature muffin cups and press the pastry to fit the shape of the cup. Place them in the oven and bake 6 minutes, or until golden brown and crisp.

2. Meanwhile, cut the chicken into small dice. Heat the oil in a large frying pan. Add the chicken and cook, stirring occasionally, until it begins to brown, about 5 minutes. Stir in the salsa and cook until heated through, about 1 minute.

3. When the pastry cups are done, remove them from the oven and fill with the chicken mixture. Garnish each cup with a sprig of cilantro.

MAKES 12

SMOKED TURKEY AND CORNED BEEF ROLL-UPS

Rolled into cylinders and seasoned with a spicy mustard filling, these easy appetizers are like enjoying a favorite deli sandwich—without the bread! They can also be turned into attractive canapés. To do so, chill for an hour or so and slice crosswise into ½-inch-thick pinwheels. Place each pinwheel on a buttered slice of cocktail rye. You can get about 6 pinwheels from each roll, so this recipe could make around 6 dozen canapés, if you are so inclined.

1 package (8 ounces) cream cheese, softened
2 tablespoons horseradish mustard
12 thin slices of corned beef (about 6 ounces)
12 thin slices of smoked turkey (about 6 ounces)

1. In a small bowl, work the cream cheese and mustard until smooth.

2. Place a slice of corned beef on top of a slice of smoked turkey, trimming the meats so they are the same size, if necessary. Spread about 1 heaping tablespoon of the cream cheese mixture over the corned beef. Roll up the meats into a tight cylinder. Repeat with the remaining meats and cream cheese. Pass immediately or refrigerate until serving time.

MAKES 12

ZUCCHINI ROUNDS WITH HAM MOUSSE

Using a pastry bag is the fastest and most decorative way to assemble this appetizer. Garnish each one with a caper, a small sprig of parsley, a tiny piece of red pepper or a light dusting of sweet paprika.

¼ pound Black Forest or honey-baked ham
1 package (8 ounces) cream cheese
1 tablespoon lemon juice
2 medium zucchini

1. Cut the ham into cubes and place them in a food processor. Pulse several times to chop the ham coarsely. Add the cream cheese, and lemon juice and process until smooth.

2. Trim the ends off the zucchini and cut crosswise into ⅜-inch rounds.

3. Place the mousse in a pastry bag fitted with a star tip. Pipe about 1½ teaspoons of mousse on each zucchini round.

MAKES ABOUT 36

Broccoli and Salami Frittata

1 package (10 ounces) thawed frozen chopped broccoli
3 ounces salami
2 tablespoons olive oil
8 large eggs
$1/2$ teaspoon salt
$1/4$ teaspoon freshly ground pepper
$1/2$ cup shredded mozzarella cheese

1. Preheat the broiler. Squeeze the broccoli to remove as much moisture as possible. Coarsely chop the salami.

2. In a large nonstick frying pan with a heatproof handle, heat the oil over high heat. Add the broccoli and salami and cook, stirring often, until any excess moisture has evaporated from the broccoli, about 3 minutes.

3. In a medium bowl, beat the eggs, salt and pepper. Reduce the heat to medium and add the eggs to the frying pan. Use a spatula to lift up the cooked edges of the frittata while you tilt the pan to allow the uncooked portion to flow underneath. Continue cooking in this manner until the edges are firm, 3 or 4 minutes. (The top will still be uncooked, but will cook further in the broiler.)

4. Sprinkle the mozzarella cheese over the top of the frittata. Broil about 3 inches from the heat until the top is set and the cheese is melted, 1 to 2 minutes. Cut into wedges and serve warm or at room temperature.

6 to 8 servings

SIMPLE SOPES

This recipe was created one day when we craved Mexican *sopes*—bite-size masa shells piled with a spicy filling—but only had ten minutes. The secret to making them so quickly turned out to be refrigerated Chinese won ton wrappers and a can of spicy chili. Don't use designer lettuce here. Iceberg lends the right amount of crunchiness.

12 won ton wrappers (about 3 inches square)
1 can (15 ounces) chili
3 radishes
¼ cup finely shredded iceberg lettuce
3 tablespoons sour cream

1. Preheat the oven to 400 degrees F. Place the won ton wrappers in miniature muffin cups and press the pastry to fit the shape of the cup. Place them in the oven and bake about 6 minutes, until golden brown and crisp.

2. Meanwhile, pour the chili into a microwave-safe bowl. Cover and cook on High for 2½ to 3 minutes, stirring once, until the chili is heated through.

3. While the chili is heating, rinse the radishes. Trim each end and cut lengthwise in half, then thinly slice.

4. When the pastry cups are done, remove them from the oven and spoon in the chili. Garnish each with about 1 tablespoon of shredded lettuce and a tiny dollop of sour cream. Top with a few radish slices. Serve while the chili is still hot.

MAKES 12

CRISPY FISH WITH
SPICY RED SAUCE

A generous dose of horseradish added to bottled cocktail sauce creates a lively dip for crisp fish cubes. To save time, shake the fish cubes with the crumbs in a plastic bag to coat quickly.

1 pound red snapper or other firm white fish fillets
1 cup Italian-style seasoned bread crumbs
2 eggs
$1/4$ teaspoon salt
$1/4$ teaspoon freshly ground pepper
1 tablespoon prepared white horseradish
$1/2$ cup bottled red cocktail sauce

1. Preheat the oven to 475 degrees F. Cut the fish into 1-inch cubes. Pour the crumbs into a plastic bag. Crack the eggs into a shallow bowl. Season with salt and pepper, then beat with a fork until blended.

2. Place half of the fish cubes in the eggs and stir gently. With a slotted spoon, remove the cubes and place them in the plastic bag. Shake a few seconds to coat the fish with the crumbs. Place the fish cubes on a greased baking sheet. Bread the remaining fish in the same fashion.

3. Bake the fish cubes 4 minutes. Then transfer to the broiler about 4 inches from the heat and broil about 3 minutes longer, or until the fish is white and opaque throughout and the crumbs are brown. Stir the horseradish into the cocktail sauce and serve as a dip.

6 TO 8 SERVINGS

CHIVE OMELET SPIRALS WITH SMOKED SALMON

Roll thin chive-flavored omelets around buttery slices of smoked salmon and some sour cream, then cut into bite-size pieces for an easy appetizer.

3 eggs
1 tablespoon minced chives
$1/8$ teaspoon salt
$1/8$ teaspoon pepper
1 tablespoon butter
4 thin slices of smoked salmon
$1/4$ cup sour cream

1. Lightly beat the eggs and chives together in a small bowl. Season with the salt and pepper.

2. Heat an 8-inch nonstick frying pan over medium-high heat. Add one-fourth of the butter. When the butter starts to sizzle, pour in one-fourth of the egg mixture to make a thin layer. Swirl to coat the pan. Cook just until the egg is set, then turn out onto a plate or board. Repeat to make 3 more egg sheets.

3. Place a slice of smoked salmon over the bottom part of 1 egg sheet. Spoon 1 tablespoon of sour cream down the center of the salmon and roll the omelet up into a cylinder. Fill the remaining omelets. Chill if you aren't serving them immediately. To serve, cut each omelet roll into 6 pieces.

MAKES 24

CUCUMBER WITH SMOKED SALMON

Crisp slices of cool green cucumber are topped with a dab of creamy dill mustard mayonnaise and a bite of smoked salmon in this appetizer. Buy fresh dill, if you can; it imparts more flavor, and you'll have a few sprigs of feathery green leaves to add for garnish.

1 large cucumber
$1/2$ cup mayonnaise
2 tablespoons chopped fresh dill, plus a few sprigs for garnish
2 teaspoons Dijon mustard
3 ounces thinly sliced smoked salmon

1. Trim the ends from the cucumber. Pare, leaving several thin strips of the dark green peel showing. Then cut the cucumber into $3/8$-inch rounds.

2. In a small bowl, blend the mayonnaise with the chopped dill and mustard. Spoon about 1 teaspoon of the dill mayonnaise on each cucumber slice.

3. Roll the slices of salmon up and cut into $3/8$-inch pieces. Stand a piece of rolled salmon on top of the dill sauce on each cucumber slice. Garnish with a sprig of fresh dill. Serve immediately or refrigerate to serve later.

MAKES ABOUT 24

ARTICHOKE BOTTOMS WITH FETA CHEESE AND SHRIMP

It's worth going out of your way to find artichoke bottoms. You can usually find jars or cans of them in well-stocked delis, Italian markets, specialty food shops and in some supermarkets. Mild in flavor, they can be stuffed with a variety of fillings.

2 cans (13¾ ounces each) artichoke bottoms
⅔ cup cooked shelled baby shrimp
4 ounces crumbled feta cheese
2 tablespoons diced pimiento
1 tablespoon chopped fresh parsley

1. Drain the artichoke hearts and arrange them on a serving platter.

2. Place the shrimp, feta cheese, pimiento and parsley in a medium bowl and toss lightly until the ingredients are combined. Spoon about 1 tablespoon of the filling into the cavity of each artichoke heart. Serve slightly chilled or at room temperature.

6 TO 8 SERVINGS

Baby Shrimp in Endive

If you have access to the newer red-leafed varieties of Belgian endive, buy one head of each variety and alternate the red- and green-tinged leaves on the serving platter for a visually striking presentation. To keep endive from becoming too bitter, be sure to refrigerate it, wrapped in a paper towel inside a plastic bag, and use within a day or two.

2 heads of Belgian endive
3 green onions
½ pound cooked shelled baby shrimp
¼ cup finely chopped red bell pepper
1 tablespoon lemon juice

1. Separate the heads of endive into individual leaves. Arrange them on a platter with the tips of the leaves pointed toward the center of the platter.

2. Trim the green onions. Finely chop the white part and half of the green. In a medium bowl, toss the chopped green onions with the shrimp, bell pepper and lemon juice.

3. Place a spoonful of the shrimp mixture in the wide part of each endive leaf.

4 TO 6 SERVINGS

DEVILED CHICKEN NUGGETS

These crispy chicken cubes deftly seasoned with mustard and Tabasco are always a hit at parties.

3 slices of firm-textured white bread
1 pound skinless, boneless chicken breasts
$1/4$ cup Dijon mustard with tarragon
$1/4$ cup dry white wine
$1/2$ teaspoon Tabasco
$1/2$ teaspoon salt
$1/4$ teaspoon freshly ground black pepper

1. Preheat the broiler. In a food processor, grind the bread to crumbs. Cut the chicken into 1-inch squares. In a medium bowl, whisk together the mustard, wine and Tabasco. Add the chicken and stir to coat evenly. Season the bread crumbs with the salt and pepper. Pour half of the bread crumbs into a shallow pie plate.

2. Quickly roll some of the chicken in the crumbs to coat all over. Place the chicken on a greased baking sheet. Bread the rest of the chicken, adding more crumbs as needed.

3. Broil about 4 inches from the heat for about 4 minutes, until golden brown. Turn them over with a wide spatula and brown the other side for 3 to 4 minutes longer. Remove to a platter and serve with toothpicks.

6 TO 8 SERVINGS

SHRIMP MOUSSE ON CUCUMBERS

Use a pastry bag to pipe a decorative dollop of this savory mousse on top of each cucumber slice. If you don't have one handy, a resealable plastic bag can be an adequate substitute. Just fill the bag with the mousse mixture and seal. Then cut the tip off one of the corners and pipe the mousse through.

3 green onions
1 package (3 ounces) cream cheese, at room temperature
1 pound cooked shelled baby shrimp
    Juice from 1 lemon (about 3 tablespoons)
1 English (hothouse) seedless cucumber, about 10 inches long

1. Trim the green onions and cut them into 2-inch lengths. Place them in a food processor and pulse several times to chop coarsely.

2. Add the cream cheese and pulse several times to mix. Add the shrimp and lemon juice and puree until creamy and smooth.

3. Rinse the cucumber, pat dry and cut into slices about ¼ inch thick. Arrange the cucumber slices on a serving platter. Place the mousse in a pastry bag and pipe about 1 tablespoonful on top of each cucumber slice. Or spoon mousse on top.

8 SERVINGS

Spicy Pickled Shrimp

Here's a wonderful pickled shrimp recipe that's hard to resist. Although you can serve it immediately, it's even better if the shrimp are allowed to cool in the pickling brine. It's easy to double or triple the recipe as needed.

1 cup dry white wine
2/3 cup lemon juice
2 tablespoons mixed pickling spices
1/2 teaspoon crushed red pepper
2 pounds shelled and deveined medium-large shrimp
(20 to 25 per pound)

1. Pour the wine and lemon juice into a medium nonreactive saucepan. Stir in the pickling spices and red pepper flakes. Cover and bring to a boil over high heat.

2. Stir in the shrimp. Cover again and cook until the liquid returns to a boil and the shrimp turn bright pink and curl, about 3 minutes. Remove from the fire and let the shrimp stand in the brine for 3 to 4 minutes. Strain off the pickling spices and serve with toothpicks.

6 to 8 servings

3 CANAPÉS, TOASTS AND CRISPS

It's amazing what you can do with a slice of bread, crisp cracker, won ton wrapper, pita pocket, tortilla chip or prebaked pizza crust as a base for a savory topping. The canapés, appetizer toasts and savory crisps in this chapter will give you some idea.

The great thing about bread-based appetizers is that they are so versatile and can be quite economical. This category of appetizers provides an outlet for using leftover sliced meats and cheeses.

Featured here are cold canapés based on special flavor pairings, such as prosciutto and pears or salami and fennel. There are also recipes for popular hot canapés, including Artichoke Cheese Canapés and Cheddar Cheese Puffs. In addition, you'll find a selection of mouthwatering pizza bites and Chinese Shrimp Toasts.

To prevent the bread from becoming soggy, it's best not to make canapés too far in advance. That's no problem with these recipes. Even if time is tight, they can all be made in 10 minutes or less.

FENNEL AND CARAWAY CRISPS

It only takes a few minutes to turn refrigerated won ton wrappers into fabulous homemade crackers. And it's a good thing, too, considering how fast these cheesy fennel and caraway seed crisps disappear. Using a wide pastry brush makes it easy to spread the oil on the pastry quickly.

24 won ton skins (about 3 inches square)
1½ tablespoons olive oil
¼ cup grated Parmesan cheese
2 tablespoons fennel seeds
1 tablespoon caraway seeds

1. Preheat the oven to 400 degrees F. Line 2 baking sheets with parchment or foil. With a sharp knife, cut the stack of won ton wrappers in half diagonally into triangles. Arrange the won ton triangles in a single layer on the baking sheets with the edges close together but not touching.

2. Brush the won ton skins lightly with the olive oil. Sprinkle the cheese, fennel seeds and caraway seeds evenly over the triangles.

3. Bake about 6 minutes, until the triangles are golden brown and crisp. Use a wide spatula to remove them to a serving tray. Serve warm or at room temperature.

MAKES 48

ZESTY GARLIC BREAD

In Gilroy, California, the garlic capital of the world, people believe that you can't get too much of a good thing. This recipe will surely please all serious devotees of the stinking rose. If you like, sprinkle some grated Parmesan or Romano cheese on top before popping the bread under the broiler.

1 stick (½ cup) butter
¼ cup finely chopped parsley
1 tablespoon minced garlic
¾ teaspoon crushed hot red pepper
1 loaf (1 pound) French bread

1. Preheat the broiler. Melt the butter in the microwave oven on High for about 1 minute. Stir in the parsley, garlic and hot pepper.

2. Slice the bread in half horizontally. Brush or spoon the garlic butter over the cut sides of the bread. Place the bread on a baking sheet and broil 3 to 4 inches from the heat about 3 minutes, until nicely toasted. Cut into 1-inch pieces and serve.

4 TO 6 SERVINGS

ARTICHOKE CHEESE CANAPÉS

This simple canapé always gets rave reviews. It's not necessary to buy freshly grated cheese for this recipe. In fact, it's better to use cheese from the can.

½ cup mayonnaise
½ cup grated Romano cheese
12 marinated artichoke heart halves
24 thin slices of baguette (narrow French bread) or 2-inch rounds cut out of white bread

1. Preheat the broiler. In a small bowl, combine the mayonnaise and cheese, stirring until well blended. Cut the artichoke pieces in half.

2. Arrange the slices of bread on a baking sheet and broil 3 to 4 inches from the heat 1 to 2 minutes, until lightly browned. Turn the slices over and remove from the broiler for a moment.

3. Spread the cheese mixture over the slices of bread to the edge. Top each with a piece of marinated artichoke heart.

4. Return the bread to the oven and broil about 2 minutes, until the topping begins to bubble and starts to brown around the edges. Watch carefully so the canapés don't burn.

MAKES 24

ARTICHOKE AND SUN-DRIED TOMATO SCONES

These savory bite-size scones are ideal for afternoon tea or with cocktails. Lining your baking pan with a sheet of parchment will save you time, especially during the cleanup.

2 cups buttermilk baking mix
1 teaspoon dried basil
$1/2$ cup milk
$1/2$ cup marinated artichoke hearts, drained
$1/4$ cup slivered sun-dried tomatoes packed in oil, drained

1. Preheat the oven to 450 degrees F. Combine the buttermilk baking mix and basil in a medium bowl.

2. Measure the milk into a large measuring cup. Coarsely chop the artichoke hearts and stir into the milk along with the sun-dried tomatoes.

3. Pour the milk mixture over the baking mix and stir just until all the ingredients are moistened. Drop heaping teaspoonfuls of dough onto a parchment-lined or buttered baking sheet.

4. Bake in the middle of the oven 8 to 10 minutes, until the scones begin to brown. Serve warm.

MAKES 18

TOASTED OLIVE CANAPÉS

This is one of my favorite hot appetizers. It's quick, pretty and has an appealing crisp texture contrasted by a soft savory topping.

1/2 cup freshly grated Parmesan cheese
1/2 cup mayonnaise
1/2 cup finely sliced green onions
1 can (2 1/4 ounces) sliced ripe olives
16 slices of cocktail rye bread

1. Preheat the oven to 475 degrees F. Combine the Parmesan cheese, mayonnaise and green onions. Drain the olives and stir them into the cheese mixture.

2. Generously spread the olive cheese mixture on top of the bread, using a rounded tablespoon for each. Arrange on a baking sheet and place in the oven for about 6 minutes, until the bottoms are brown and the tops begin to turn golden brown. Serve immediately.

MAKES 16

PESTO PIZZA

There used to be a popular San Francisco pizza parlor that was renowned for two very different reasons. The first was that it shared space with a Chinese restaurant. The second was the house specialty: pesto pizza. To duplicate it, all you need is a high-quality, ready-to-use crust, some basil, garlic, olive oil and good Parmesan cheese.

1½ cups packed fresh basil leaves
  2 garlic cloves, crushed
  ⅓ cup extra virgin olive oil
  ½ cup grated Parmesan cheese
  ¼ teaspoon salt, or to taste
  ¼ teaspoon freshly ground pepper
  2 individual-size (7- to 8-inch), ready-to-use pizza crusts

1. Preheat the oven to 450 degrees F. In a food processor or blender, combine the basil leaves, garlic, olive oil, ¼ cup of the cheese and the salt and pepper. Process, scraping the bowl down once or twice, until the mixture is fairly smooth, about 3 minutes. Spread the pesto over the pizza crusts.

2. Sprinkle the remaining ¼ cup cheese over the pizzas. Bake about 8 minutes, until the crust is brown and the cheese melts. Cut into 8 wedges each and serve hot.

4 OR 5 SERVINGS

Crostini with Fresh Tomatoes and Kalamata Olives

When fresh tomatoes are in season, we enjoy them every way possible. In this tasty appetizer, thin slices of juicy sweet tomatoes, tangy Kalamata olives and a few anchovies are drizzled with fruity olive oil and served warm on French bread.

6 English muffins
3 tablespoons extra virgin olive oil
3 medium-size ripe tomatoes
½ jar (7 ounces) pitted Kalamata olives, coarsely chopped (½ cup)
2 tins (2 ounces each) flat fillets of anchovies

1. Preheat the broiler. Split each English muffin in half. Lightly brush olive oil on the cut side of each English muffin half and arrange, cut sides up, on a baking sheet.

2. Cut each tomato into 4 slices. Place 1 slice of tomato on each muffin half. Scatter the Kalamata olives over the tomatoes. Drape 2 anchovy fillets over each muffin. Drizzle the remaining olive oil over the tomatoes.

3. Place the crostini under the broiler 3 to 4 inches from the heat and broil 3 to 5 minutes, until the tomatoes are heated through. Serve immediately.

MAKES 12

CANAPÉS WITH SUN-DRIED TOMATOES AND BASIL

Crisp melba toasts or water crackers are delicious topped with herbed goat cheese, plump marinated sun-dried tomatoes and fresh basil. For variation, use a dollop of pesto instead of the fresh basil.

    1 package (5 ounces) wheat melba toast
 1/2 pound herb-flavored or pepper goat cheese
    1 large cucumber
 15 sun-dried tomato halves packed in oil
 15 fresh basil leaves

1. Spread each piece of melba toast with herb-flavored goat cheese.

2. Peel the cucumber; cut it into 30 thin slices. Place 2 slices of cucumber and 1 sun-dried tomato half on top of each piece of melba toast and garnish with a fresh basil leaf. Serve immediately.

MAKES 15

CALIFORNIA PIZZA

Every time we think there can't be another pizza, a new place opens with another innovation. Here's mine. Both the tapenade (black olive paste) and the roasted pepper are available in jars.

2 individual-size (7- to 8-inch), ready-to-serve pizza crusts
1/3 cup tapenade
1 package (5 ounces) herb-flavored goat cheese
1 whole roasted red pepper
2 small zucchini

1. Preheat the oven to 450 degrees F. Place the pizza crusts on a baking sheet. Spread a thin layer of tapenade over both pizza crusts.

2. Crumble the goat cheese and scatter it on top of the tapenade. Cut the red pepper into thin strips. Thinly slice the zucchini. Scatter the red pepper strips and zucchini slices over the pizza crust.

3. Place the pizzas on the bottom oven rack and bake 8 minutes, or until the crust is brown and the toppings are heated through. Serve hot, cut into wedges.

3 OR 4 SERVINGS

CHEDDAR CHEESE PUFFS

Here is one easy use for a little bit of leftover beer. Of course, you can always open a new bottle and drink the rest. Rounds of cocktail pumpernickel or rye bread also work well here.

12 (2-inch diameter) circles cut out of white bread
1 cup shredded sharp Cheddar cheese
2 egg yolks
$^1/_4$ cup beer

1. Preheat the broiler. Place the slices of bread on a baking sheet. Broil 3 to 4 inches from the heat about 1$^1/_2$ minutes, until the bread begins to brown. Remove the bread from the oven and reduce the oven temperature to 375 degrees F.

2. Meanwhile, place the cheese in a 1-quart glass measuring cup. Microwave on High about 40 seconds to soften. Remove from the microwave and vigorously stir in the egg yolks and beer until the mixture is fairly smooth.

3. Spread a layer of the cheese mixture on each slice of bread, covering the bread completely. Bake for 8 minutes, or until the cheese topping begins to puff. If desired, run under the broiler 1 minute to brown the top. Serve immediately.

MAKES 12

PEAR AND BLUE CHEESE PIZZA

The classic dessert combo—sweet fresh pears and creamy blue cheese—join here in an unusual warm appetizer. Drizzling honey on the pears brings out their flavor and also does something wonderful for blue cheese.

4 ounces double-cream blue cheese, at room temperature
2 individual-size (7- to 8-inch), ready-to-use pizza crusts
2 fresh ripe pears
1 tablespoon wildflower or other honey
1 teaspoon dried thyme leaves

1. Preheat the oven to 425 degrees F. Spread the blue cheese on the pizza crusts. Core the pears and cut them lengthwise into thin slices. Arrange the slices of pear on top of the cheese. Drizzle with the honey and sprinkle ½ teaspoon thyme over each pizza.

2. Bake the tarts on the bottom rack of the oven about 8 minutes, until heated through. Then place under the broiler for 1 to 2 minutes longer to brown the pears lightly. Cut each tart into 8 wedges and serve warm.

4 OR 5 SERVINGS

Chicken Tostaditas

Use the flat, round, nacho-style corn chips as a base for appetizer tostaditas. For variety you can also garnish them with sliced ripe olives, diced tomato or a dollop of pureed avocado.

1 can (16 ounces) vegetarian refried beans
1 pound skinless, boneless chicken breasts
$1/4$ cup salsa verde
24 round tortilla chips
$1/2$ cup sour cream

1. Spoon the beans into a glass bowl and microwave on High for $2^{1}\!/_{2}$ minutes to heat through. Cut the chicken crosswise into $1/2$-inch-wide strips.

2. Heat a large heavy frying pan over high heat for about 1 minute. Pour the salsa verde into the hot frying pan. Immediately add the chicken and cook over high heat, stirring occasionally, until the chicken is cooked through and no longer pink, about 4 minutes.

3. While the chicken is cooking, arrange the nacho chips on a large serving platter. Top each chip with a rounded tablespoon of the beans. When the chicken is done, top each chip with 3 to 4 strips of the chicken mixture and a dollop of sour cream. Serve hot.

MAKES 24

CHEESY CHILE TOAST

This easy hors d'oeuvre is always a company favorite. If you like bolder flavors, use hot pepper Jack instead of plain Monterey Jack cheese and sprinkle a light dusting of crushed hot red pepper on top before serving.

1 can (7 ounces) diced green chiles
1 package (8 ounces) shredded Monterey Jack cheese
3/4 cup minced red bell pepper
1/2 cup mayonnaise
8 slices of French, English muffin or white bread

1. Preheat the broiler. Drain the chiles and combine them in a medium bowl with the cheese, bell pepper and mayonnaise. Stir until well blended.

2. Arrange the bread in a single layer on a baking sheet. Broil 3 to 4 inches from the heat about 2 minutes, until brown. Turn the bread over and spread the cheese mixture over the bread.

3. Return to the broiler and broil about 4 minutes longer, until the cheese melts and begins to brown. Watch carefully to be sure it doesn't burn. Cut each slice of bread into quarters and serve warm.

6 TO 8 SERVINGS

FONTINA TOASTS WITH SWEET PEPPERS

Here's an updated version of the classic grilled cheese sandwich that makes a delicious snack or savory hot appetizer. You can also cook this sandwich in a sandwich grill or even a waffle iron.

3 to 4 ounces fontina cheese
4 slices of country-style whole wheat bread
1 whole marinated sweet red pepper
1 tablespoon pesto
1 tablespoon olive oil

1. Thinly slice the cheese and cut it to fit the bread. Arrange the cheese on 2 slices of bread. Cut the pepper into strips and arrange them on top of the cheese. Spread ½ tablespoon pesto over each of the other 2 slices of bread and place them, pesto side down, on top of the peppers to form sandwiches.

2. Brush the olive oil over the outside of all 4 slices of bread. Place the sandwiches on a hot griddle or in a preheated frying pan and weigh down with a heavy pan. Cook over moderate heat, turning once, until the cheese melts and the sandwich is golden brown on both sides, about 5 minutes. Cut into triangles to serve.

2 SERVINGS

CANAPÉS WITH PROSCIUTTO AND PEARS

Salty cured prosciutto has a special affinity for sweet, juicy pears. Both are combined with sage butter in these easy canapés. If you decide to assemble them ahead of time, squirt a little lemon juice over the pear slices to prevent browning.

3 tablespoons butter
1 tablespoon chopped fresh sage leaves or 1 teaspoon crumbled dried sage
24 thin slices of baguette (narrow French bread), cut about ³/₈ inch thick
2 to 3 ripe pears
12 thin slices of prosciutto

1. Soften the butter. Add the sage, stirring and mashing until well blended. Spread some of the sage butter over each slice of bread.

2. Halve the pears and cut out the cores. Cut each pear half into 6 thin wedges. Cut each slice of prosciutto crosswise in half.

3. To assemble the canapés, mound a piece of prosciutto on top of each slice of bread and top with a wedge of pear.

MAKES 24

SALAMI AND FENNEL CANAPÉS

Tangy slices of hard salami and crisp, anise-flavored fresh fennel are another one of those special flavor combinations. Here they are paired with a tart lemony mayonnaise on crisp rounds of melba toast. You could also use thin slices of a seeded baguette (narrow French bread) or 2-inch rounds cut out of thinly sliced French bread.

1 lemon
$1/3$ cup mayonnaise
30 thin melba snack rounds
30 thin slices of hard salami
1 small bulb of fresh fennel

1. Grate the outermost colored zest from the lemon. Squeeze the juice from $1/2$ of the lemon. Combine the mayonnaise, lemon zest and juice. Spread some of the mixture on each of the melba snack rounds.

2. Fold the slices of salami almost in half and place them on the melba rounds.

3. Trim the stems and leaves off the top of the fennel (reserve the feathery leaves to use in other recipes). Trim off the bottom and any wilted outer layers. Thinly slice the fennel bulb, cutting away the core, then cut the slices into thin strips. Arrange 2 or 3 fennel strips on top of each piece of salami and serve.

MAKES 30

SALMON-STUFFED PITA POCKETS

Whoever decided to downsize pita breads must have had appetizers in mind. For this savory snack, mini whole wheat pitas are filled with thin slices of dilled Havarti and an easy salmon salad. Then they are baked until the cheese melts and the bread is crisp. These little bites are also good cold.

1 can (14³/₄ ounces) pink salmon
1 large plum tomato
6 green onions
¹/₂ pound Havarti with dill
6 small whole wheat pita breads (about 4 inches in diameter)

1. Preheat the oven to 450 degrees F. Drain the salmon and place it in a medium bowl; flake with a fork. Cut the tomato into ¹/₂-inch dice. Finely chop the green onions. Stir the tomatoes and green onions into the salmon.

2. Thinly slice the cheese. Split each pita horizontally into 2 rounds. Place 6 rounds (insides up) on a baking sheet. Top each with sliced cheese and about ¹/₃ cup of the salmon mixture. Cover with the remaining rounds of pita (insides down) and press down slightly.

3. Bake about 7 minutes, until the cheese melts and the bread is crisp. Cut into quarters to serve.

6 SERVINGS

SARDINE SMORREBROD SANDWICHES

In Denmark, *smorrebrod,* open-face sandwiches, are an art form. Made in miniature, they become wonderful appetizers. You can use any cold sliced meat or smoked fish as the focus. A few thin slices of red onions would be an additional nice garnish. Herring can be substituted for the sardines.

2 tablespoons unsalted butter
6 slices of cocktail pumpernickel bread or other firm-textured
   bread
6 small leaves of butter lettuce
2 plum tomatoes
1 tin (3³/₄ ounces) lightly smoked sardines in olive oil

1. Soften the butter and spread it on the bread. Arrange a lettuce leaf on each slice of bread.

2. Thinly slice the tomatoes and place 1 slice on top of each lettuce leaf. Top with a smoked sardine and serve.

MAKES 6

SHRIMP QUESADILLAS

Flour tortillas substitute beautifully for homemade pancakes in this quick snack. Tahini, Middle Eastern sesame paste, holds a savory green onion and shrimp filling for the tortillas. Occasionally tahini separates on standing. If so, just stir until smooth.

4 flour tortillas (9 inches in diameter)
1/4 cup tahini
4 green onions
1/2 cup cooked shelled baby shrimp
  Salt
1 cup vegetable oil

1. Place the tortillas on a flat surface. Brush or spread 1 tablespoon tahini over each tortilla, covering almost to the edges.

2. Thinly slice the green onions. Sprinkle the sliced green onions and shrimp over 2 of the tortillas. Season lightly with salt. Top with the other 2 tortillas, tahini side down, and press firmly together.

3. Heat the oil in a 10-inch frying pan. When the oil is hot, slide in one of the tortilla cakes and fry, pressing down with a spatula, until the bottom is golden brown. Turn over and brown the other side. Remove and drain on paper towels. Cook the other tortilla cake. Cut each into 8 wedges and serve warm.

4 SERVINGS

SHRIMP TOASTS

1 bunch of green onions (about 6)
1 pound shelled and deveined raw shrimp
1½ tablespoons Thai fish sauce
¼ teaspoon salt
12 slices of firm-textured white bread
2 cups vegetable oil

1. Trim the roots off of the green onions. Cut the white bottoms and 3 inches of the green leaves into 1-inch lengths. Place in a food processor and pulse several times to chop them. Add the shrimp, fish sauce and salt and process to a paste, about 1 minute.

2. Stack 6 slices of bread. With a serrated knife, trim the crusts off the bread. Then cut the bread diagonally in half into triangles. Repeat with the remaining bread.

3. Pour the oil into a large deep frying pan and heat to about 375 degrees F. While the oil is heating, spread 1 rounded tablespoon of the shrimp paste on each bread triangle.

4. When the oil is hot, add the bread triangles, shrimp side down, and fry, turning once, until golden brown on both sides, about 2 minutes. Remove with a slotted spoon and drain on paper towels. Serve warm.

MAKES 24

4 ELEGANT BUT EASY

Some days you want to splurge on ingredients or to make a statement with your presentation. This chapter features appetizers that are a little special. In some cases, the recipes may use foods that are slightly more expensive or require a bit of effort to find. But just because an appetizer is elegant doesn't mean it's difficult to prepare. On the contrary, all of the recipes in this chapter can be whipped up in 10 minutes or less just before the first guest rings the doorbell.

Delicacies, such as tiny New Potatoes with Crème Fraîche and Caviar, Avocado Pancakes with Crabmeat and Sweet Corn and Shrimp Cakes, are just the thing to serve when you want to pull out all the stops. Eggplant Roulades with Goat Cheese and Red Peppers or Mini Steak au Poivre make truly special starters to a gourmet dinner.

Look through this chapter next time a client is coming to dinner and you want to impress her.

BLACK BEAN CAKES

The secret to making these savory appetizer pancakes in 10 minutes instead of in several hours is using canned black beans. If you can, buy a brand that's seasoned with salt and onions. Garnish with dollops of sour cream and salsa.

1 can (15 ounces) black beans
1/4 cup flour
1 egg
1/4 teaspoon salt
1/2 cup sour cream
1/2 cup salsa

1. Drain the beans and place them in a food processor. Process until smooth, about 1 minute; scrape down the sides of the bowl. Add the flour, egg and salt and process 30 seconds, until well blended.

2. Preheat a nonstick or lightly oiled griddle. Make pancakes using 1 tablespoon of batter for each and spreading the batter out slightly with the back of a spoon to about 2 inches in diameter. Cook in batches over medium-high heat until the bottom is brown and a few bubbles appear on top, about 2 minutes. Turn the pancakes over and cook until the other side is lightly browned, 1 to 2 minutes. Garnish with dollops of sour cream and salsa.

4 TO 6 SERVINGS

EGGPLANT ROULADES WITH GOAT CHEESE AND RED PEPPERS

1 medium eggplant (about 1 pound)
1 tablespoon olive oil
4 small jarred roasted red peppers
1/3 cup goat cheese
4 teaspoons pine nuts
   Salt and pepper

1. Peel the eggplant with a paring knife or swivel-bladed vegetable peeler. Slice lengthwise into 4 (3/8-inch) slices measuring about 6 inches long and 3 inches wide. (You'll only need half of the eggplant for this recipe. Save the rest to use another time.)

2. Heat the oil in a large frying pan over high heat. Arrange the eggplant slices in a single layer in the pan and cook, turning, about 2½ minutes per side, until the eggplant is golden brown and tender.

3. Meanwhile, drain the peppers. Cut 2 of them in half and place the 4 halves on a flat surface. Spread the goat cheese over the peppers and sprinkle 1 teaspoon of pine nuts over each. Place the remaining peppers in a blender and process until smooth.

4. When the eggplant is done, remove it from the pan and season with salt and pepper to taste. Place a pepper on top of each eggplant slice and roll up. Divide the sauce among 4 plates. Arrange the eggplant rolls on top of the sauce. Serve at room temperature.

4 SERVINGS

Mushrooms in Madeira

Use fresh wild mushrooms when they are available or a combination of wild and cultivated mushrooms. Serve on toast points or in pastry shells for an elegant but easy first course.

1 pound medium mushrooms
2 large shallots
2 tablespoons butter
$1/3$ cup Madeira
$1/2$ cup heavy cream
$1/4$ teaspoon salt
$1/4$ teaspoon freshly ground pepper

1. Cut the mushrooms in half. Finely chop the shallots. In a large frying pan, melt the butter over high heat. Add the shallots and sauté until softened and fragrant, about 1 minute. Add the mushrooms and cook, stirring occasionally, until the mushrooms begin to soften, about 3 minutes. Transfer the mushrooms to a bowl.

2. Pour the Madeira into the frying pan and bring to a boil, scraping up any browned bits from the bottom of the pan. Boil until reduced by half, 1 to 2 minutes. Add the cream and boil over high heat, stirring occasionally, until the sauce thickens, 3 to 4 minutes. Pour the sauce over the mushrooms. Season with the salt and pepper.

4 SERVINGS

NEW POTATOES WITH CRÈME FRAÎCHE AND CAVIAR

You can cook tiny new potatoes quickly in the microwave oven. Topped with crème fraîche and caviar, they make an elegant hurry-up hors d'oeuvre. To ensure even cooking, select potatoes that are approximately the same size. (You can also use slightly larger potatoes but they'll take a little more time to cook.)

3/4 pound small new potatoes (1 to 1 1/2 inches in diameter)
1/2 cup crème fraîche or sour cream
2 ounces golden caviar or lumpfish roe
1 tablespoon minced chives

1. Rinse the potatoes and place them in a circle in a shallow round, microwave-safe casserole. Pour in 2 tablespoons water and cover the casserole tightly. Microwave on High for 5 minutes, or until the potatoes are tender. (The cooking time may vary slightly depending on the size of the potatoes.) Let stand 2 minutes. Then carefully uncover.

2. Cut each potato in half and arrange them, cut sides up, on a serving tray. (You may have to cut a thin slice off the bottom so they don't roll around.) Top with dollops of crème fraîche and caviar. Garnish with the minced chives and serve.

MAKES ABOUT 24

SWEET POTATO CROWNS

To save time here, you can buy cooked, crumbled real bacon bits in jars.

1 medium-size sweet potato or yam (about 2½ inches in diameter and weighing about ½ pound)
1 tablespoon minced chives
⅓ cup sour cream
3 tablespoons crumbled cooked bacon

1. Trim the ends off the sweet potato. Peel, then cut it into thin slices, each about ¼ inch thick.

2. On a microwave-safe platter, arrange the slices in a circular pattern with a few in the center. Cover with microwave-safe plastic wrap and microwave on High for about 5 minutes, until the potatoes are cooked through but not too soft. Let stand 1 minute. Then uncover and arrange the slices on a serving platter.

3. Stir the chives into the sour cream. When the potatoes have partially cooled, top each slice with a dollop of the chive sour cream and about ½ teaspoon of crumbled bacon. Serve warm or at room temperature.

MAKES ABOUT 16

BANDERILLAS

These little kebabs, a specialty at Spanish tapas bars, provide a wonderful way to use up leftover bits of tasty foods. All you need do is thread about five different tastes on a small skewer. Some possibilities besides the one suggested below include: cooked asparagus tips, cocktail onions, gherkins, cooked shrimp, a folded piece of salami, an anchovy rolled around a large caper, a blanched broccoli floret. The trick is to put everything in your mouth at one time to savor the flavors together.

12 marinated artichoke hearts
12 cubes of Black Forest or honey-baked ham
12 ears canned baby corn
12 pimiento-stuffed olives
12 (1-inch) squares red bell pepper

1. Thread an artichoke heart, a piece of ham, an ear of baby corn, a stuffed olive and a bell pepper square on a cocktail toothpick or small skewer. Repeat for the remaining ingredients, changing the order of the ingredients on different skewers.

2. Arrange all of the skewers on a platter and serve slightly chilled or at room temperature.

MAKES 12

Prosciutto-wrapped Asparagus with Orange Mint Mayonnaise

If you want a more pronounced orange flavor in the mayonnaise, stir in a teaspoon of freshly grated orange zest. This light hors d'oeuvre can be served as finger food or it can be plated as a first course.

24 asparagus spears
12 thin slices of prosciutto
$^2/_3$ cup mayonnaise
 2 tablespoons orange juice
 2 tablespoons chopped fresh mint

1. Trim off the large ends from the asparagus to leave 6-inch tips. (If you like, reserve the stems of the asparagus for soup.) In a large frying pan, bring 1 inch of water to a boil over high heat. Add the asparagus and cook until just tender, 2 to 3 minutes. Drain and rinse under cold running water. Drain well and pat dry.

2. Cut each slice of prosciutto in half and roll around an asparagus spear. Arrange on a serving platter.

3. Stir together the mayonnaise, orange juice and mint and serve alongside the asparagus as a dipping sauce.

MAKES 24

PORK TENDERLOIN WITH GLAZED CURRIED APPLES

Thin slices of pork topped with wedges of glazed apples makes a pretty appetizer to serve on small plates or on thin rounds of French bread. To save time, use an apple corer/slicer to divide the apple quickly into wedges.

1 well-trimmed pork tenderloin (about 8 to 9 ounces)
1/4 teaspoon salt
1/4 teaspoon freshly ground pepper
1 red-skinned apple
1 tablespoon butter
1/2 teaspoon curry powder
1 tablespoon mango chutney

1. Preheat the broiler. Cut the pork into 16 thin slices and flatten each slice slightly with the palm of your hand. Season the pork with the salt and pepper and arrange the slices on a broiler pan. Core the apple, then cut it into 16 wedges.

2. In a medium frying pan, melt the butter over medium-high heat. Stir in the curry powder and cook 30 seconds. Add the apple wedges and cook, turning once, about 3 minutes, until the apples begin to soften.

3. Place the meat under the broiler 3 to 4 inches from the heat and broil 4 to 5 minutes, until white throughout but still moist. Brush the chutney on the pork and top each slice with a wedge of apple. Return to the broiler for 1 minute to glaze.

4 TO 6 SERVINGS

Lamb Noisettes Flavored with Herbed Mint Butter

When you want to splurge for a special occasion, treat yourself to lamb noisettes, little nuggets of boneless loin of lamb. Best of all, these cook in minutes, 8 minutes in a 500 degree F. oven or less than 5 minutes in a cast-iron skillet over high heat.

5 tablespoons butter, softened
10 ounces boneless loin of lamb
    Salt and pepper
1½ teaspoons dried herbes de Provence
1½ teaspoons chopped fresh mint
20 thin slices of seeded baguette (narrow French bread)

1. Melt 2 tablespoons of the butter in a large heavy frying pan, preferably seasoned cast-iron, over medium-high heat. Add the lamb and cook, turning, until nicely browned outside and medium-rare inside, about 4 minutes. Remove the meat to a cutting board. Season with salt and pepper to taste.

2. In a small bowl, blend 3 tablespoons butter, with the herbes de Provence and mint. Spread over the bread. Slice the meat thinly and place one slice on each slice of bread. Serve warm or at room temperature.

MAKES 20

MINI STEAK AU POIVRE

Sometimes favorite entrées served in small portions work well as appetizers or first courses. That's the case with this quick version of the popular steak in pepper sauce. It's best to serve it on a plate with toast points to soak up the delicious juices.

10 ounces well-trimmed center cut beef tenderloin
$1/4$ teaspoon salt
  1 tablespoon green peppercorns
  1 tablespoon butter
$1/4$ cup dry red wine
  2 tablespoons heavy cream

1. Cut the meat into $1/4$-inch-thick slices. Season with the salt. Press the peppercorns into the slices. Any that don't adhere will become part of the sauce.

2. Heat the butter in a large frying pan over high heat. Add the slices of meat and cook, turning once, until rare, 30 to 60 seconds per side.

3. Remove the meat from the pan and pour in the wine. Stir briskly to loosen any browned bits from the bottom of the pan. Stir in the cream. To serve, place 3 slices of meat on each of 4 small plates and pour a small amount of the sauce over the steak.

4 SERVINGS

BAKED STUFFED CLAMS

This is a wonderful quick way to serve fresh clams. Unless you are unusually adept at shucking clams, ask your fishmonger to open the clams for you and leave them on the half shell. I like to serve these with lemon wedges on the side.

2 dozen cherrystone clams on the half shell
2 garlic cloves
1 cup Italian-seasoned bread crumbs
$1/4$ cup grated Parmesan cheese
$3^{1}/_{2}$ tablespoons olive oil

1. Preheat the oven to 425 degrees F. Arrange the clams on a broiler pan. Mince the garlic.

2. In a small bowl, blend together the bread crumbs, Parmesan cheese, garlic and olive oil. Mound the stuffing over the clams.

3. Bake 5 to 7 minutes, until the topping is lightly browned. Serve while hot.

6 SERVINGS

STEAMED CLAMS WITH FENNEL

Bits of fresh fennel add a slight anise flavor to this easy first course. You may want to serve each guest a slice or two of garlic toast so they can sop up all the delicious juices.

2 pounds small manila or littleneck clams
1 large shallot
2 garlic cloves
1/2 cup coarsely chopped fresh fennel
1 1/2 cups dry white wine

1. Scrub the clams well. Mince the shallot and garlic. Place the minced shallot and garlic in a large saucepan. Add the fennel, wine and 1/2 cup water. Cover the pan and cook over medium-high heat until the mixture comes to a boil, about 3 minutes.

2. Add the clams and cover tightly. Let steam until the clams open, about 5 minutes.

3. To serve, divide the clams among 4 soup bowls. Then tip the pan and ladle out the fragrant broth and vegetables, being careful not to include any sand that might be at the bottom of the pan.

4 SERVINGS

APPETIZER CRAB CAKES

These miniature crab cakes are delicious served cold or hot and crispy. Cooked crabmeat, which is easier to find than fresh uncooked crabmeat, works fine in this recipe. You can also use canned crabmeat here.

$1/2$ pound crabmeat
3 green onions
3 tablespoons seasoned dry bread crumbs
2 eggs
$1/4$ teaspoon salt
$1/4$ teaspoon freshly ground pepper
$1 1/2$ to $2 1/2$ tablespoons olive oil

1. Flake the crabmeat and place it in a bowl. Trim the root off the green onions and rinse well. Finely chop the white bulb and about 2 inches of the green leaves. Add the chopped green onions, bread crumbs, eggs, salt and pepper to the crabmeat. Stir to blend well.

2. Heat $1 1/2$ tablespoons oil in a large frying pan. Add the crabmeat in batches, allowing about 1 tablespoon for each cake. Fry until golden brown and crisp on the bottom, about 2 minutes. Turn over and cook until the other side is golden brown, about 2 minutes longer. If necessary, add more oil to the pan when you cook the next batch. Serve immediately or chill and serve cold.

6 SERVINGS

AVOCADO PANCAKES
WITH CRABMEAT

Serve this elegant appetizer as a passed hors d'oeuvre or arrange 3 on each plate for a first course. Using freshly opened beer adds a pleasant yeasty flavor and lightness to the pancake batter. An avocado peeler, which scoops out half an avocado in one piece, leaving the peel behind, will allow you to prepare the avocados in a flash.

2 small avocados (about 6 ounces each)
1/2 cup buttermilk baking mix
3/4 cup beer
1/2 cup sour cream
1/4 pound cooked crabmeat

1. Cut the avocados in half. Remove the pits and peel; then thinly slice both avocados.

2. Preheat a nonstick or lightly oiled pancake griddle. In a small bowl, whisk together the buttermilk baking mix and beer until smooth. When the griddle is hot, make pancakes using 1 tablespoon batter for each. With the back of the spoon, spread the batter out slightly to make a 2-inch circle. Top each pancake with 2 or 3 slices of avocado. When the bottom is nicely browned, about 2 minutes, turn over and cook the other side until lightly browned, 1 to 2 minutes. Repeat until all the batter is used.

3. Serve pancakes, avocado side up, garnished with a dollop of sour cream and a tablespoon of crabmeat.

6 SERVINGS

MUSSELS IN SAFFRON CREAM

Mussels make tasty appetizers, served hot with saffron-scented cream. Buy farm-raised mussels, if possible, to save time scrubbing and debearding them.

2 large shallots
²/₃ cup dry white wine
2 pounds scrubbed and debearded mussels (about 36)
¹/₄ teaspoon saffron threads
1 cup heavy cream

1. Chop the shallots. Combine the shallots and wine in a large nonreactive saucepan. Cover and bring to a boil over high heat.

2. Add the mussels. Cover tightly and let steam just until the mussels open, about 3 minutes. With a slotted spoon, transfer the mussels to 6 soup bowls and cover to keep warm. Discard any mussels that don't open.

3. Strain the mussel liquid, discarding any grit at the bottom. Rinse the saucepan and return the liquid to the pan. Add the saffron and cream. Boil over high heat, stirring occasionally, until the sauce thickens slightly, 4 to 5 minutes. Pour the saffron cream over the mussels and serve at once.

6 SERVINGS

GREMLINS ON HORSEBACK

You've probably heard of angels on horseback (bacon-wrapped oysters) and devils on horseback (bacon-wrapped oysters enlivened with hot pepper sauce). Now there's gremlins on horseback—what we call scallops and jicama wrapped in bacon. If jicama is not available, substitute whole or halved water chestnuts.

1 small jicama
12 slices of bacon
1 pound sea scallops
$\frac{1}{2}$ cup apricot preserves
1$\frac{1}{2}$ teaspoons soy sauce

1. Preheat the broiler. Peel the jicama with a paring knife. Cut into $\frac{1}{2}$-inch-thick slices. Then cut the slices into 1-inch squares. You'll need 24 pieces. Cut each strip of bacon in half. If the scallops are very large, cut them in half.

2. Place a scallop in the center of a piece of bacon. Top with a piece of jicama and bring the ends of the bacon over the jicama. Place seam side down on a baking sheet. Repeat with the remaining scallops, bacon and jicama.

3. In a small bowl, stir together the apricot preserves and soy sauce. Set the dipping sauce aside.

4. Broil the wrapped scallops 3 to 4 inches from the source of heat 4 to 5 minutes, until the bacon is crisp and the scallops are just opaque throughout. Remove and drain on paper towels.

MAKES ABOUT 24

OYSTER SPINACH PACKAGES

Serve this appetizer on small plates. You can also wrap the oysters in butter lettuce leaves.

2 large shallots
1 cup dry white wine
2 jars (10 ounces) shucked oysters in their own juice or 16 or
    18 freshly shucked oysters
16 or 18 large leaves of fresh ready-to-use spinach
1½ sticks unsalted butter

1. Chop the shallots. Place the shallots and white wine in a large nonreactive frying pan and bring to a boil over high heat. Boil until the wine is reduced by half, about 4 to 5 minutes.

2. Drain the oysters and wrap a spinach leaf around each one.

3. When the wine has reduced, reduce the heat to medium and whisk in the butter, 2 tablespoons at a time. When all of the butter has been incorporated, place the oyster packages, seam side down, in the sauce. Cook gently, spooning the sauce over the oysters several times, until the oysters are slightly firm, about 3 minutes.

4. Serve immediately, placing the oysters on plates with some of the sauce.

4 TO 6 SERVINGS

SALMON FILLET WITH RED PEPPER COULIS

For this pretty first course, the salmon is sliced on the bias as it would be for smoked salmon. Ask your fishmonger to slice six 2-ounce portions for you. You may want to garnish the plates with a sprig of parsley, some fresh herbs or a few watercress leaves.

1 cup roasted sweet red peppers (available in jars)
$1/4$ cup clam juice
$1/8$ teaspoon hot pepper sauce, or more to taste
6 flat slices of skinless salmon fillet, each weighing about
    2 ounces
$1/4$ teaspoon salt
$1/8$ teaspoon freshly ground pepper
1 tablespoon olive oil

1. Place the roasted peppers and clam juice in a blender or food processor and puree until smooth. Season with the hot sauce.

2. Season the salmon with the salt and pepper. Heat the oil over high heat in a large frying pan. Add the pieces of salmon and cook about $1\frac{1}{2}$ minutes per side, until just opaque throughout.

3. Pour about 2 tablespoons of the red pepper sauce onto each plate; spread the sauce out in a larger circle with the back of your spoon. Place the salmon on top of the sauce and serve.

6 SERVINGS

SALMON WRAPPED IN GRAPE LEAVES WITH LEMON CAPER SAUCE

This appealing first course proves that pickled grape leaves have a use beyond dolmas.

1 pound center-cut salmon fillet
8 pickled grape leaves
5 tablespoons butter, melted
1 tablespoon lemon juice
2 teaspoons tiny (nonpareil) capers

1. Preheat the broiler. Cutting straight down, slice the salmon fillet crosswise into 8 strips, each about 1 inch wide and 5 inches long.

2. Remove the stems from the grape leaves. Place a grape leaf on a flat surface. Arrange a salmon strip in the center of the leaf and then bring the sides of the leaf up and over to partially cover the salmon. (If the leaves are very large, you'll want to cut them in half.) Wrap the rest of the fish the same way and place the packets on a broiler pan.

3. Lightly brush some of the melted butter over the fish and place it under the broiler about 3 inches from the heat. Broil about 5 minutes, until the fish is just opaque throughout.

4. Stir the lemon juice and capers into the remaining melted butter. Serve the salmon packets on appetizer plates and spoon some of the lemon caper butter over each portion.

SMOKED SALMON AND HERB TERRINE

This is a showstopping, sophisticated first course. Many supermarkets carry 3-ounce packages of smoked salmon slices, which are the perfect length for a mini-loaf pan. The terrine comes together in a snap, but should be chilled for a few hours to firm the layers. Freeze to hasten the chilling. Serve with thinly sliced pumpernickel bread, garnished with watercress sprigs.

4 ounces plain cream cheese, softened
1/2 cup packed watercress leaves, finely chopped
6 ounces thinly sliced smoked salmon
4 ounces chive-flavored cream cheese spread, softened

1. Place a piece of plastic wrap inside a 6- by 3 1/2-inch mini-loaf pan, letting the excess hang over the sides. In a small bowl, work the plain cream cheese and watercress until well blended.

2. Place 2 slices of smoked salmon, trimmed and overlapping to fit the pan as needed, in the bottom of the pan. Spread with half of the watercress cream cheese. Top with another layer of smoked salmon. Spread with half of the chive cream cheese. Continue layering with salmon, the remaining watercress cream cheese, a fourth layer of salmon, the remaining chive cream cheese and then a final layer of salmon. Bring up the plastic wrap to wrap the terrine tightly and press down to compress the layers.

3. Refrigerate until completely chilled, at least 3 hours. To serve, remove from the pan, unwrap and slice crosswise with a sharp thin-bladed knife into 8 slices. Serve chilled.

4 SERVINGS

SHRIMP WITH
FERMENTED BLACK BEANS

You can find fermented black beans, a popular Chinese condiment, in well-stocked supermarkets and Asian grocery stores. Made from black beans that have been preserved in a salty brine often seasoned with ginger and citrus peel, they last indefinitely stored in a jar in the refrigerator. Although they're generally rinsed before being used, the salty brine brightens the flavor of this quick first course.

1½ tablespoons olive oil
  2 garlic cloves
  3 tablespoons fermented black beans
  1 pound large shrimp (20 to 25 count), shelled and deveined
 ¼ cup dry white wine

1. Heat the oil in a large frying pan. Run the garlic through a garlic press into the pan. Cook over medium heat, stirring, until the garlic begins to turn golden, 30 to 60 seconds.

2. Stir in the black beans and shrimp. Cook over medium heat, stirring, until the shrimp are pink and loosely curled, about 3 minutes.

3. Add the wine and bring to a boil. Divide the shrimp and sauce among 4 appetizer plates.

4 SERVINGS

SWEET CORN AND SHRIMP CAKES

Of all the recipes for corn cakes that I've tried or tasted, this is the easiest and one of the tastiest. Serve them plain or, if you like, garnish with a dollop of tart green salsa made from tomatillos. Thawed frozen corn works well in this recipe.

3 cups corn kernels (fresh or thawed frozen)
2 tablespoons flour
1 egg
$^1/_4$ cup heavy cream or milk
$^1/_2$ teaspoon salt
$^1/_2$ cup cooked shelled baby shrimp

1. Puree 2 cups of the corn in a food processor. Add the flour, egg, cream and salt and pulse several times to combine. Stir in the rest of the corn and the shrimp.

2. Heat a nonstick or lightly oiled griddle. Make corn cakes using 1 tablespoon of batter for each. Cook in batches over medium-high heat until the bottoms are nicely browned, about 2 minutes. Turn over and cook the other sides until lightly browned, $1^1/_2$ to 2 minutes longer. Serve immediately.

6 TO 8 SERVINGS

SESAME BUTTERFLY SHRIMP

In just a few minutes, you can serve these deep-fried seafood treats with a crisp sesame seed crust. For a sweet and spicy dip, add a dollop of prepared hot Chinese mustard to a bowl of prepared duck sauce.

3 cups vegetable oil
1 pound large shrimp (20 to 25 count), shelled and deveined, tail segment left intact
2 large egg whites
⅓ cup sesame seeds

1. Heat the oil in a medium saucepan until it reaches 375 degrees F.

2. Using a small knife, cut the shrimp down the center almost but not completely through. Spread the shrimp open to "butterfly."

3. In a medium bowl, beat the egg whites until foamy. Add the shrimp and toss well to coat. Place the sesame seeds in a small bowl. Holding the shrimp by the tail, dip one side of each shrimp in the sesame seeds.

4. In batches, fry the shrimp until golden brown, about 2 minutes. Remove with a slotted spoon and drain on paper towels.

4 TO 6 SERVINGS

GARLIC SHRIMP TAPAS

Tapas, Spanish hors d'oeuvres, used to be found only in the bars of the Iberian peninsula, but now are popular in this country as well. Here's one of the best known tapas, quickly sautéed shrimp in a heady garlic and sherry sauce. Sprinkle with chopped parsley and serve with baguette slices for sopping up the sauce.

2 garlic cloves
3 tablespoons butter
1 pound shelled and deveined large shrimp (20 to 25 count)
1/3 cup dry sherry
2 tablespoons lemon juice
1/4 teaspoon salt
1/4 teaspoon freshly ground pepper

1. Mince the garlic. In a medium frying pan, melt 2 tablespoons of the butter over medium-high heat. Add the shrimp and garlic and cook, stirring often, until the edges of the shrimp are turning pink, about 1 minute.

2. Add the sherry, lemon juice, salt and pepper and cook until the shrimp are just completely pink and firm, about 2 minutes longer. Remove from the heat and swirl in the remaining 1 tablespoon butter.

3. Transfer the shrimp and sauce to small individual bowls (custard molds work well) and serve hot.

4 SERVINGS

5 Marvelous and Meatless

Fruits and vegetables make delicious—often low-calorie and low-fat—appetizers, especially when they are enjoyed at their peak of ripeness. With today's interest in lighter, more healthful eating, most people are looking to produce stores and farmers' markets for inspiration and are cooking with the seasons.

This chapter features a wide variety of cold hors d'oeuvres, such as Curried Snow Peas with Peanuts and Asparagus Spears with Sesame Mayonnaise, which can be put together quickly at the last minute. Many of them, Bocconcini, marinated bite-size cubes of fresh mozzarella, for example, can be made ahead and will only improve in the refrigerator.

You'll also find some creative hot hors d'oeuvres here. Straw Potato Pancakes, Old-Fashioned Corn Fritters and Pesto-stuffed Mushrooms always get rave reviews.

With recipes like these, guests will undoubtedly ask for seconds. They may even ask for thirds. The only thing they won't ask is "Where's the beef?"

ASPARAGUS SPEARS WITH SESAME MAYONNAISE

This is a delicious but light starter to serve before a heavy meal.

1 pound asparagus spears
Salt
²/₃ cup mayonnaise
2 tablespoons soy sauce
1 teaspoon Asian sesame oil
Grated zest of 1 orange

1. Pour about 1 inch of water into a large frying pan and bring it to a boil over high heat. Meanwhile, cut off the tough bottom ends from the asparagus. Generously salt the boiling water. Add the asparagus, return the water to a boil and cook until the asparagus is just tender, about 3 minutes. Drain the asparagus and rinse under cold running water. Drain well and pat dry.

2. In a small bowl, combine the mayonnaise, soy sauce, sesame oil and grated orange zest. Blend well. Spoon the dipping sauce into a small bowl. Place the bowl in the middle of a round platter and fan the asparagus spears on the platter around it.

4 TO 6 SERVINGS

CARROT, JICAMA AND ORANGE SALAD

Throughout Mexico and Central America, cocktail hour begins with the refreshing arrival of a platter of jicama sticks and orange sections sprinkled with lime juice, chili powder and salt. Sometimes carrot and cucumber sticks, honeydew and watermelon spears are included as well.

1 medium jicama (about 1 pound)
3 carrots
2 oranges or tangerines
2 limes
1 teaspoon chili powder
$1/2$ teaspoon salt

1. Peel the jicama and cut it into spears about $2^{1}\!/_{2}$ by $^{1}\!/_{2}$ inch. Peel the carrots and cut them into sticks about $2^{1}\!/_{2}$ by $^{1}\!/_{2}$ inch. Peel the oranges, then separate them into sections. Cut 1 lime into wedges.

2. Arrange the jicama, carrots and orange sections on a platter. Garnish with the lime wedges. Squeeze the juice from the other lime over the fruit and vegetables. Dust with the chili powder and salt. Serve slightly chilled or at room temperature.

6 SERVINGS

TURKISH CARROTS

A variation of this intriguing dish often shows up on *mezze,* or appetizer, tables in Turkey. If you like, garnish the platter with lightly toasted whole almonds. Although this mixture is traditionally served as a salad, it's also delicious spread on thinly sliced French bread or scooped up in pita. The quickest way to grate the carrots is in your food processor using the finest shredding disk.

3/4 pound carrots
1 large garlic clove
1 tablespoon olive oil
1/2 teaspoon salt
1/2 cup nonfat plain yogurt

1. Peel the carrots and shred them in the food processor fitted with the finest shredding disk. Mince the garlic.

2. Heat the oil in a large frying pan over medium-high heat. Add the garlic and sauté until soft and fragrant, about 30 seconds. Stir in the carrots and season with salt. Cook, stirring occasionally, until the carrots soften and turn bright orange, about 6 minutes. Remove the carrots from the heat.

3. Fold the yogurt into the carrots. Serve warm or chill and serve cold.

MAKES 2 CUPS

OLD-FASHIONED CORN FRITTERS

Featherlight, piping hot, bite-size corn fritters are a winning passed hors d'oeuvre. If you like added zest, stir in one seeded and minced fresh jalapeño pepper. To make a quick dip, heat honey until slightly thinned, then stir in a dash of bourbon.

3 cups vegetable oil
1 large egg
1 (8½-ounce) can cream-style corn
⅔ cup self-rising flour
¼ teaspoon salt

1. Heat the oil in a large saucepan until it reaches 375 degrees F.

2. In a medium bowl, beat the egg and stir in the corn, flour and salt just until blended. In 2 or 3 batches, drop heaping teaspoons of the batter into the hot oil. Fry, nudging the fritters with a wooden spoon to turn halfway through cooking until golden brown, about 3 minutes. Remove with a slotted spoon and drain on paper towels. Serve hot.

6 TO 8 SERVINGS

KOREAN CUCUMBERS

English or hothouse cucumbers are great for a quick hors d'oeuvre because they are sweet-flavored and virtually devoid of any bitter seeds. This Asian-inspired marinade shows off the cucumbers' delicate flavor.

   1 tablespoon soy sauce
   1 teaspoon sugar
  1/4 teaspoon sesame chili oil
   1 English (hothouse) cucumber, about 10 inches long
1 1/2 teaspoons toasted sesame seeds

1. In a medium-size bowl, combine the soy sauce, sugar and sesame chili oil.

2. Rinse the cucumber and pat dry. Trim the ends. Cut the cucumber in half lengthwise, then cut each half into pieces about 1/2 inch long. Add the cucumber pieces to the marinade, stirring gently, until the cucumbers are well coated with the marinade. Let stand for 5 to 10 minutes.

3. Sprinkle the sesame seeds over the cucumber slices and serve with toothpicks.

4 TO 6 SERVINGS

PESTO-STUFFED MUSHROOMS

Prepared pesto sauce, which you can find in the refrigerated section of your supermarket, makes these tasty stuffed mushrooms unbelievably quick and easy.

16 medium mushrooms
$1/4$ cup basil pesto
2 tablespoons bread crumbs
2 tablespoons grated Parmesan cheese
$1 1/2$ tablespoons pine nuts

1. Preheat the oven to 400 degrees F. Twist off the mushroom stems and reserve for another use. Place the caps, cavity side up, in a baking dish.

2. In a small bowl, stir together the pesto and bread crumbs. Stuff the cavity of each mushroom with 1 heaping teaspoon of the pesto filling. Sprinkle the Parmesan cheese and a few pine nuts on top of each mushroom.

3. Bake 7 minutes, or until the mushrooms are heated through and the nuts begin to brown. Serve while hot.

MAKES 16

TEXAS CAVIAR

We eat black-eyed peas every New Year's because they symbolize prosperity and good fortune. We eat them many other times during the year just because we like them. Even people who claim not to care for them fill up on this delicious vegetarian dip. Serve it with corn tortilla chips or warm pita triangles.

1 can (15 ounces) black-eyed peas
3 green onions
2 garlic cloves
$1/2$ cup thick and chunky red tomato salsa (medium-hot)
3 tablespoons finely chopped cilantro

1. Rinse the black-eyed peas and drain them well. Pour them into a serving bowl.

2. Trim away the root ends of the green onions. Cut them in half lengthwise, then thinly slice. Mince the garlic.

3. In a small dry frying pan, toast the cumin seeds over medium heat, shaking the pan often, until they darken and become fragrant, 2 to 3 minutes. Gently fold the green onions, toasted cumin seeds, salsa and cilantro into the peas and serve.

MAKES 2 CUPS

CURRIED SNOW PEAS WITH PEANUTS

These sweet, crisp green snow peas half covered with curried cheese and chopped peanuts look beautiful on cold appetizer trays. They taste even better than they look.

24 fresh snow peas
2/3 cup dry-roasted peanuts
4 ounces cream cheese, softened
1 1/2 tablespoons mango chutney
1/2 teaspoon curry powder

1. Remove the strings from the snow peas. Rinse them and pat dry. Finely chop the peanuts.

2. In a small bowl, beat together the cream cheese, chutney and curry powder until well blended. Place the peanuts in a shallow bowl or soup plate.

3. Spread a small amount of the curried cheese on one end of each snow pea and dip them in the peanuts to coat.

4 TO 6 SERVINGS

STRAW POTATO PANCAKES

Top these crisp potato pancakes with dollops of sour cream and applesauce, if you like.

1 russet potato (½ pound)
1 small yam or sweet potato (about 4 ounces)
1 egg
2 tablespoons flour
½ teaspoon salt
¼ teaspoon freshly ground pepper
2 to 3 tablespoons vegetable oil

1. Peel the potato and the yam. Then shred them in the food processor using the fine shredding disk. Place them in a bowl and cover with cold water. After 30 seconds, drain them, squeezing as much of the water out as possible.

2. Preheat a griddle or 2 large frying pans. In a medium bowl, beat the egg until blended. Add the potatoes and mix well. Stir in the flour, salt and pepper.

3. Oil the griddle or frying pans. Form potato pancakes using 1 heaping tablespoon of the potato mixture for each and flattening them slightly. Cook about 4 minutes, until the bottom side is golden brown. Brush the top with oil and turn over. Cook about 4 minutes longer, or until the potatoes are tender and the bottom is brown. Serve hot.

3 OR 4 SERVINGS

POTATO AND PARMESAN FRITTATA

Slice these golden frittatas into wedges and served warm on plates as a lovely first course. Or you can cool a frittata to room temperature and cut it into 1-inch pieces as finger food appetizers.

2 tablespoons olive oil
3 cups (12 ounces) thawed frozen potatoes O'Brien
8 eggs
³/₄ teaspoon dried oregano
¹/₂ teaspoon salt
¹/₄ teaspoon freshly ground pepper
¹/₄ cup freshly grated imported Parmesan cheese

1. Preheat the broiler. In a large nonstick frying pan with a heatproof handle, heat the oil over high heat. Add the potatoes O'Brien and cook, stirring often, until they are lightly browned, about 5 minutes.

2. In a medium bowl, beat the eggs, oregano, salt and pepper. Reduce the heat to medium and add the eggs to the frying pan. Use a rubber spatula to lift up the cooked edges of the frittata, and tilt the pan to allow the uncooked portion to flow underneath. Continue cooking in this manner until the edges are firm, about 4 minutes. (The top will still be uncooked, but will cook further under the broiler.)

3. Sprinkle the Parmesan cheese over the top of the frittata. Broil about 3 inches from the heat 1 to 2 minutes. Cut into wedges and serve warm or at room temperature.

6 TO 8 SERVINGS

FRIED GREEN TOMATOES

4 small green tomatoes (about 2 inches in diameter)
1 cup yellow cornmeal
1 teaspoon dried sage
1/4 teaspoon salt
1/4 teaspoon freshly ground black pepper
3 tablespoons vegetable oil
1/4 cup grated Parmesan cheese

1. Preheat the broiler. Rinse the green tomatoes and cut them into 1/2-inch-thick slices. In a shallow bowl, combine the cornmeal, sage, salt and pepper. Dredge the tomatoes in the seasoned cornmeal, turning to coat both sides.

2. Heat half the oil in a large frying pan over medium-high heat. Add half of the tomatoes and cook, turning once, until golden brown on both sides, 2 to 3 minutes. Remove the tomatoes from the pan and place them on a broiler pan. Fry the rest of the tomatoes in the remaining oil.

3. Sprinkle the Parmesan cheese over the fried green tomato slices. Broil about 4 inches from the heat for 1 to 2 minutes to brown the cheese.

4 SERVINGS

CRISPY ZUCCHINI STICKS

This is one of the most popular items on bar appetizer menus across the country. Using herb-flavored stuffing mix as a coating gives the fried zucchini extra crunch. Sprinkle on seasoned salt or grated Romano cheese before serving.

1 pound small zucchini (about 5)
2 cups herb-flavored stuffing mix
2 eggs
2 cups vegetable oil
3/4 teaspoon seasoned salt or 1/4 cup grated Romano cheese

1. Rinse the zucchini and pat dry. Cut the tip off each end, then cut into lengthwise halves. Slice each half into 3 long strips.

2. Place the stuffing mix in a blender or food processor and pulse several times until the crumbs are fine. Pour them into a shallow bowl or pie plate. Break the eggs into another pie plate and whip with a fork.

3. Dip the zucchini in the eggs and then in the crumbs, turning to coat all sides.

4. Heat 1 inch of oil in a large frying pan until it reaches 375 degrees F. Fry the zucchini in several batches until golden brown and crispy, about 1 1/2 minutes per batch. Remove with a slotted spoon and drain on paper towels. Sprinkle with seasoned salt or cheese and serve hot.

3 TO 4 SERVINGS

BOCCONCINI

Cut fresh mozzarella into bite-size cubes and season them with garlic, fruity olive oil, oregano and red pepper flakes for this homemade seasoned *bocconcini*. You can assemble this appetizer ahead and keep it in the refrigerator. It only gets better.

2 pounds fresh mozzarella
6 large garlic cloves
$\frac{1}{2}$ cup extra virgin olive oil
2 tablespoons dried oregano
$\frac{1}{2}$ to $\frac{3}{4}$ teaspoon crushed hot red pepper

1. Cut the mozzarella into 1-inch cubes. Coarsely chop the garlic. Combine the garlic and olive oil in a large bowl. Stir in the oregano and hot pepper.

2. Add the mozzarella cubes and toss gently until the cheese is well coated with the oil and seasonings. Serve with toothpicks.

8 TO 10 SERVINGS

MOZZARELLA CHEESE CHUNKS WITH MARINARA SAUCE

½ pound mozzarella cheese
2 eggs
1½ cups Italian seasoned bread crumbs
½ teaspoon salt
¼ teaspoon pepper
2 cups vegetable oil
½ cup prepared meatless marinara sauce

1. Slice the cheese in half. Then cut each half into quarters. Break the eggs into a shallow bowl and beat them lightly with a fork until blended. Pour the bread crumbs into another shallow bowl and mix with the salt and pepper.

2. Dip the cheese into the eggs and then into the bread crumbs, turning to coat all sides. Repeat the process to add a second layer of crumbs. Let the cheese dry on a piece of wax paper for a minute or so while the oil heats.

3. Pour the oil into a medium-size saucepan and heat over high heat until it reaches 375 degrees F. To be sure the oil is hot enough, drop a bread crumb into it; the oil should start to sizzle immediately. Fry the cheese for 1 to 2 minutes, until golden brown on all sides and melted.

4. While the cheese is frying, heat the marinara sauce. Serve the cheese cubes at once with the warm marinara sauce for dipping.

8 SERVINGS

PESTO POLENTA BITES

Spread pesto over polenta and top with sliced tomatoes for a colorful and savory appetizer.

3 tablespoons extra virgin olive oil
6 medium tomatoes
1 tablespoon salt
1 package (17 ounces) quick-cooking polenta
1½ cups grated Parmesan cheese
1 cup basil pesto

1. In a large saucepan, bring 2 quarts of water to a full boil. Meanwhile, brush 1 tablespoon of the oil over the bottom and sides of a 10½- by 15½-inch jelly roll pan. Cut the tomatoes into ¼-inch slices; then cut the slices in half.

2. When the water begins to boil, stir in the remaining oil and the salt. Remove the pan from the heat and stir in all of the polenta, beating with a whisk or wooden spoon.

3. Return the polenta to the heat and cook over medium-high heat, stirring until thick, 5 minutes. Stir in the cheese, blending well. Pour the polenta into the oiled pan; smooth the top with a spatula.

4. Spread the pesto over the polenta. Arrange the tomato slices on top of the pesto. Cut into 1½-inch squares to serve.

MAKES 70 PIECES

THREE CHEESE POLENTA

With the availability of quick-cooking polenta, you can whip up a large batch of savory polenta appetizers in a hurry. Serve these polenta bites warm or at room temperature. If you like, make the polenta in advance, then reheat it as you need it either by running it under the broiler or sautéing pieces in a frying pan.

3 tablespoons butter
1/4 pound fontina cheese
2 teaspoons salt
1 package (17 ounces) quick-cooking polenta
1/4 pound grated Parmesan cheese
1/4 pound blue cheese, such as Roquefort or Maytag

1. In a large saucepan, bring 2 quarts of water to a full boil. Meanwhile, use 1 tablespoon of the butter to butter a 10½- by 15½ -inch jelly roll pan. Finely dice the fontina.

2. When the water begins to boil, add the salt. Remove the pan from the heat and stir in the polenta, beating with a whisk or wooden spoon. Return to the heat and cook over medium-high heat, stirring, until thick, about 5 minutes. Beat in the remaining butter. Immediately spread the polenta in the buttered pan.

3. Preheat the broiler. Sprinkle the fontina and Parmesan cheese over the polenta. Crumble the blue cheese over all. Broil about 3 inches from the heat for 1 to 2 minutes, until the cheeses melt. Cut into 1½-inch squares when ready to serve.

MAKES 70 PIECES

QUESADILLAS WITH BRIE AND PAPAYA

This is an easy way of making appetizer quesadillas. I like the contrast of the nutty Brie and the mildly sweet papaya. You can use almost anything you want for the filling as long as it's sliced very thin.

1/2 pound Brie cheese
1 papaya
8 very fresh flour tortillas (7 to 8 inches in diameter)
2 tablespoons vegetable oil

1. Preheat the oven to 475 degrees F. Thinly slice the Brie, using a sharp knife and occasionally dipping it in warm water if the cheese sticks. Cut the papaya in half and scoop out the seeds. Then peel the papaya and cut it into thin slices.

2. Brush 4 tortillas with oil and place them oiled side down on 2 baking sheets. Place 1/4 of the cheese on each tortilla. Top each tortilla with 1/4 of the papaya slices. Then top with the remaining tortillas and brush the tops with oil.

3. Bake for 4 minutes. Turn the quesadillas over and bake 2 to 4 minutes longer, until the tortillas are lightly browned and the cheese melts. Remove from the pan with a wide spatula and cut each quesadilla into 8 wedges to serve.

8 SERVINGS

QUESADILLAS WITH GARLIC JACK, GREEN CHILES AND TOMATOES

Top each wedge with a dollop of guacamole, made easily by mashing a ripe avocado with a fork and adding lemon juice and chunky salsa to taste.

8 flour tortillas (7 to 8 inches in diameter)
2 tablespoons vegetable oil
1/2 pound garlic Jack cheese
1 can (4 ounces) diced mild green chiles
2 ripe medium tomatoes

1. Preheat the oven to 500 degrees F. Brush one side of 4 tortillas with oil and place them oiled side down on 2 baking sheets. Shred the cheese. Drain the chiles and cut the tomatoes into thin slices.

2. Arrange the tomato slices over the tortillas. Then sprinkle on the cheese and the chiles. Place the remaining tortillas on top and press down firmly. Brush the tops of the tortillas with oil.

3. Bake for 4 minutes. Turn the quesadillas over and bake 2 to 4 minutes longer, until the cheese is melted and the tortillas are golden brown. Use a wide spatula to remove the quesadillas from the baking sheet to a cutting board. With a sharp knife, cut each quesadilla into 8 wedges and serve.

8 SERVINGS

PIZZA QUESADILLAS

The variety of fillings for quesadillas is limited only by the imagination. Here, the tortilla snacks take a trip to Italy with mozzarella cheese, tomatoes, basil and olives. For a variation, sprinkle each quesadilla with 2 tablespoons chopped sun-dried tomatoes instead of the fresh tomatoes.

6 (6½-inch) flour tortillas
1 cup shredded mozzarella cheese
2 ripe plum tomatoes, seeded and cut into ¼-inch dice
6 tablespoons coarsely chopped black Mediterranean olives
3 tablespoons chopped fresh basil

1. Preheat the oven to 200 degrees F. Heat a medium nonstick frying pan over medium-low heat. Place 1 tortilla in the pan. Sprinkle with ⅓ cup of the cheese, then top with ¼ cup tomatoes, 2 tablespoons olives and 1 tablespoon basil. Cook until the cheese is almost completely melted, about 1 minute.

2. Place a second tortilla over the top. Using a spatula, turn and cook until the underside is lightly browned. Place in the oven to keep warm while making 2 more quesadillas with the remaining ingredients.

3. Cut each quesadilla into 8 wedges and serve hot.

6 TO 8 SERVINGS

6 HOT AND SPICY

Since we've fallen in love with so many spicy cuisines—Mexican, Thai, and Cajun—I decided to devote an entire chapter to fiery foods. Hot and spicy food is a trend, but not a fad. It's common to find hot sauce standing next to the ketchup and cayenne beside the cinnamon in most American kitchens these days.

Today, it's as easy to find both fresh and pickled jalapeño peppers in most supermarkets as it is to locate fresh red bell peppers. There are many other ways to add a jolt of seasoning to appetizers and snacks as well. Spicy salsa, "blackened" seasoning blends and crushed hot red pepper are just a few of the ingredients that can be used to add fire and flavor to appetizers.

Among the hot and cold recipes that you'll find here are Fiery Jalapeño Artichoke Spread, Jamaican Jerked Chicken with Papaya, Chili Cheddar Wafers and Thai Fish Balls. Especially with spicy recipes like these, it's important to let your personal taste determine exactly how much to turn up the heat.

CHILI CHEDDAR WAFERS

These crisp homemade crackers have spice from chili powder and crunch from a light coating of cornmeal. Once you try them, the recipe will probably become a staple in your party repertoire.

1 stick (½ cup) butter
1 cup flour
1 cup finely shredded Cheddar cheese
2 teaspoons chili powder
½ cup yellow cornmeal

1. Preheat the oven to 475 degrees F. Cut the butter in several pieces and place in a food processor along with the flour, cheese and chili powder. Pulse several times to combine. Then process about 1 minute until the dough comes together.

2. Pour the cornmeal into a shallow dish. Pinch off small pieces of dough and roll into 24 balls about 1 inch in diameter. Drop the balls into the cornmeal and shake the dish until they are well coated. Place them 1 inch apart on an ungreased baking sheet and flatten with the bottom of a glass.

3. Bake 8 minutes, or until the bottom and edges are golden brown.

MAKES 24

CORN NACHOS

Sweet kernels of corn balance the heat of diced jalapeño peppers and taco-seasoned shredded cheese in these bite-size nachos.

1 can (4 ounces) diced jalapeño or hot chile peppers
1 small onion
1 cup corn kernels (fresh or thawed frozen)
1 cup shredded mixed cheeses with taco seasoning
32 round tortilla chips, preferably white

1. Preheat the broiler. Drain the jalapeño peppers and place them in a bowl. Finely chop the onion. Add the onion, corn and cheese to the peppers and mix gently until the ingredients are well combined.

2. Line a baking sheet with parchment or aluminum foil to facilitate the cleanup. Arrange the tortilla chips in a single layer on the baking sheet. Place about 1 tablespoon of the pepper-corn mixture on top of each tortilla chip. Broil 3 to 4 inches from the heat about 2 minutes, until the cheese melts and the chips begin to brown. Serve hot.

MAKES 32

FIERY JALAPEÑO
ARTICHOKE SPREAD

This spicy concoction is for everyone who adores bold flavors. If you like your food milder, substitute diced green chiles for the jalapeños. Slather the hot mixture on crackers, thinly sliced French or rye bread or on vegetables. It's particularly delicious on sliced cucumbers or cooked new potatoes.

1 can (13³/₄ ounces) hearts of small artichokes
1 can (4 ounces) diced jalapeños or hot chiles
²/₃ cup grated Parmesan cheese
²/₃ cup mayonnaise
1 teaspoon dried thyme

1. Preheat the broiler. Drain the artichoke hearts and chop them coarsely. Drain the jalapeño peppers. In a medium bowl, combine the chopped artichokes, jalapeños, cheese, mayonnaise and thyme. Stir until well combined.

2. Thinly spread the artichoke mixture over the bottom of an 8- or 9-inch pan that can safely go under the broiler or a large gratin pan. The dip should be no more than ¹/₂ inch thick. Broil 3 to 4 inches from the heat about 5 minutes, until the dip is heated through and golden brown on top. Serve hot.

6 TO 8 SERVINGS

MEAN BEAN DIP

There's nothing innocent about this bean dip. Scoop the zesty mixture up with crisp corn chips, warm tortillas or spears of crisp fresh vegetables, such as sweet bell peppers or jicama.

    1 can (16 ounces) refried beans
    1 can (4 ounces) diced jalapeño or hot chile peppers
    1 small onion
    2 teaspoons chili powder
1½ teaspoons ground cumin

1. Place the beans in a medium-size microwave-safe serving bowl. Drain the peppers and stir them into the beans.

2. Finely chop the onion and fold it into the bean mixture along with the chili powder and cumin. Microwave on High for about 2½ minutes, until heated through.

MAKES ABOUT 2½ CUPS

SPICY SWEET POTATO CHIPS

A light sprinkling of chili powder and garlic salt gives these sweet crunchy potato chips a pleasant bite.

4 cups vegetable oil
1 large sweet potato (about 1 pound)
3/4 teaspoon chili powder
3/4 teaspoon garlic salt
1/4 teaspoon ground red pepper, or more to taste

1. Heat the oil in a large deep frying pan to 375 degrees F. Peel the sweet potato and thinly slice in a food processor fitted with a 1 mm. slicing disk. Pat the potato slices dry on paper towels.

2. When the oil is hot, add about 1/4 of the potatoes, being careful not to crowd the pan. Cook, stirring gently to keep the potatoes from sticking to each other, until they turn golden brown and crisp, about 2 minutes. Remove them with a slotted spoon and drain on paper towels. Cook the remaining potatoes the same way.

3. Combine the chili powder, garlic salt and hot pepper and sprinkle over the potato chips before serving.

4 SERVINGS

SWEET AND SPICY PECANS

These crisp bites are irresistible and will disappear when served as a nibble with cocktails. Don't salt until after tasting, as each brand of Cajun seasoning includes different amounts of salt.

2 tablespoons butter
2 cups pecan halves
2 teaspoons Cajun seasoning
2 teaspoons sugar
  Salt to taste

1. In a medium nonstick frying pan, melt the butter over medium heat. Add the pecans and cook, stirring often, for 1 minute.

2. Sprinkle the Cajun seasoning and sugar over the nuts and cook, stirring constantly, until the sugar has melted and the nuts are glazed, about 2 minutes.

3. Transfer the pecans to a plate and cool slightly. Taste and season with salt, if needed. Serve warm or at room temperature.

6 TO 8 SERVINGS

BRIE WITH HOT PEPPER JELLY

1 wedge (8 ounces) Brie cheese
1/4 cup hot pepper jelly
1 package (8 ounces) melba toast

1. Place the wedge of Brie on a platter. Top with the hot pepper jelly.

2. Arrange slices of melba toast alongside the cheese.

4 TO 6 SERVINGS

SALSA PINWHEELS

These pinwheels are a cinch to make, but they do need a short rest
in the freezer to firm up enough to slice. Alternatively, you could
make a tortilla stack (5 layers of filling sandwiched between
6 tortillas) and cut it into thin wedges for serving. Incidentally,
the filling makes a wonderfully spicy dip for fresh vegetables.

1 package (8 ounces) cream cheese
1/2 cup thick and chunky hot tomato salsa
2 tablespoons finely chopped fresh cilantro
6 whole wheat flour tortillas (7 inches in diameter)
6 thin slices of smoked turkey (about 2 ounces)

1. If the cream cheese is hard, unwrap and microwave on High
for 15 to 30 seconds to soften. Stir in the salsa and cilantro,
blending well.

2. Spread about 1/4 cup of the filling over each tortilla. Top with a
slice of smoked turkey and roll up fairly tightly. Wrap each tortilla
roll separately in plastic wrap and place, seam side down, in the
freezer for about 5 minutes, until firm enough to slice.

3. To serve, cut into 1-inch-thick slices and arrange the pinwheels
on a platter.

MAKES ABOUT 30

MEXICAN WON TONS

Guests always give these quick appetizers rave reviews. They're very easy to make: merely fit Chinese won ton wrappers into miniature muffin tins, plop a cube of hot pepper Jack cheese into each indentation and bake until the cheese melts and the pastry is crisp. Voilà—instant party food!

12 won ton wrappers
4 ounces hot pepper Jack cheese
1/2 small ripe avocado
1 teaspoon lemon juice
1/8 teaspoon salt
12 leaves fresh cilantro

1. Preheat the oven to 425 degrees F. Press a won ton wrapper into each of 12 miniature muffin tins. Cut the cheese into 12 (3/4-inch) cubes and place 1 cube of cheese in each pastry cup. Bake for 6 to 8 minutes, until the cheese melts and the pastry is golden brown and crisp.

2. Meanwhile, peel the avocado and mash the flesh with a fork. Stir in the lemon juice and salt. When the won tons are done, remove them to a serving tray and top each with a dollop of guacamole and a cilantro leaf.

MAKES 12

SANTA FE FONDUE

Serve this snappy spread with warm flour or corn tortillas or with crisp tortilla chips.

8 ounces Monterey Jack cheese
1½ teaspoons cumin seeds
1 ripe medium tomato
2 green onions
2 tablespoons finely diced hot pickled jalapeño peppers

1. Preheat the oven to 425 degrees F. Thinly slice the cheese and place it in an 8- to 10-inch gratin dish or shallow casserole. Bake for about 8 minutes, until the cheese is melted and bubbly.

2. Meanwhile, in a small dry skillet, toast the cumin seeds over moderate heat until lightly browned and fragrant, about 3 minutes; set aside. Coarsely chop the tomato. Thinly slice the green onions.

3. Sprinkle the chopped tomato, green onions, diced jalapeño peppers and toasted cumin seeds on top of the melted cheese and serve at once.

4 SERVINGS

SASSY MINTED FRUIT

Drizzling spiced rum over wedges of juicy pineapple and oranges produces a satisfying snack that's hot and cold, sweet and tangy. Use a peeled, ready-to-use fresh pineapple to save time.

1 pound peeled and sliced fresh pineapple
1 large navel orange
¼ cup rum
¼ to ½ teaspoon Tabasco sauce
⅛ to ¼ teaspoon cayenne pepper

1. Cut the pineapple slices into thin wedges.

2. Cut the peel from the orange and then cut the orange into ¼-inch-thick slices. Cut the slices in half.

3. Arrange the pineapple wedges in a row on a serving platter. Place the orange slices on top of the pineapple. Blend the rum and Tabasco together and spoon the mixture over the fruit. Sprinkle the cayenne on top and serve chilled or at room temperature.

4 TO 6 SERVINGS

JERKED CHICKEN WITH PAPAYA

Spicy Jamaican jerk seasoning mix is increasingly available in the spice or specialty foods sections of supermarkets. In this mouthwatering appetizer, pieces of sweet tropical fruit cool the heat of the chicken. If you can't find papaya, try mango, melon cubes, fresh pineapple or even chunks of drained canned pineapple.

1 pound skinless, boneless chicken breasts
3 tablespoons jerk seasoning mix
1½ tablespoons vegetable oil
1 papaya

1. Cut the chicken into 1-inch cubes and place in a medium bowl. Add the jerk seasoning mix and toss to coat.

2. Heat the oil in a large frying pan. Add the chicken pieces and cook over medium-high heat, stirring occasionally, until the chicken is tender and begins to brown, about 5 minutes.

3. While the chicken is cooking, cut the papaya in half and remove the seeds. Then peel and cut into 1-inch cubes.

4. To serve, skewer a piece of chicken and a papaya cube together on toothpicks.

6 TO 8 SERVINGS

PÂTÉ WITH HOT AND SPICY ORANGE MUSTARD SAUCE

Although you can't make great pâté in ten minutes, you can easily jazz up a great pâté that you've purchased from your local deli or specialty food shop. This sweet-spicy sauce marries well with country-style pâté made with pork and veal. If there's any sauce left over, serve it another day with baked ham, smoked chicken or grilled pork chops.

1/2 cup orange marmalade
1 1/2 tablespoons port wine
1 1/2 teaspoons prepared hot white horseradish
1/2 teaspoon mustard seeds
1/2 pound country-style pâté

1. Combine the marmalade, port, horseradish and mustard seeds, mixing well. Spoon the sauce into a small serving bowl.

2. Cut the pâté into 4 slices. Serve the sauce on the side.

4 SERVINGS

BLACKENED PORK
WITH APPLESAUCE

There are a number of commercial "blackened" seasoning blends available today in supermarkets, and they vary in spiciness. In this tasty recipe, applesauce takes the edge off the heat.

1 well-trimmed pork tenderloin (about 8 to 9 ounces)
1½ tablespoons vegetable oil
4 teaspoons "blackened" spice seasoning blend
¾ cup chunky applesauce
4 sprigs of fresh parsley

1. Cut the pork tenderloin into 16 thin slices. Brush a light film of oil on the slices of pork. Sprinkle about ⅛ teaspoon of the seasoning blend over both sides of each slice of pork.

2. Heat a large heavy skillet, preferably cast-iron, or a grill pan over high heat until very hot. Add the slices of pork in batches without crowding, and cook, turning once, until nicely browned outside and white throughout, 2 to 3 minutes.

3. To serve, place 4 slices of pork and 3 tablespoons of applesauce on each appetizer plate. Garnish with parsley.

4 SERVINGS

THAI FISH BALLS

These traditional, slightly chewy fried fish appetizers are meant to be served warm. You can buy fish sauce at Asian markets and well-stocked supermarkets.

4 cups vegetable oil
1 pound red snapper or rockfish fillets
1 egg
1 tablespoon Asian fish sauce
3/4 teaspoon hot chili oil

1. Heat the oil in a large deep frying pan to 375 degrees F. Rinse the fish and cut each fillet into thirds. Place the pieces of fish in a food processor and pulse several times until the fish is finely chopped. Add the egg, fish sauce and chili oil and process another 30 seconds.

2. Form the fish balls by scooping up 1 teaspoon of the fish paste and pressing it along the side of the bowl to smooth it. With a second teaspoon, slide the fish balls into the hot oil and cook until golden brown and done, about 4 minutes. Repeat with the remaining mixture. (You could also wet your hands with water and roll the mixture into 1-inch balls.) Remove the fish balls from the hot oil with a slotted spoon and drain on paper towels. Serve warm.

MAKES ABOUT 24

SPICY APPETIZER SHRIMP

This recipe was given to me by my friend Ariel, who grew up in Central America. You can control the spiciness by the amount of jalapeño peppers you add. Have plenty of cold beer on ice. Serve with corn tortilla chips.

1 pound cooked shelled and deveined baby or halved
  medium shrimp
1 small red or white onion
1 lime
1 fresh jalapeño pepper
1 pickled jalapeño pepper plus 1 tablespoon of the juice
  from the jar

1. Rinse the shrimp and place them in a medium bowl. Finely dice the onion. Juice the lime. Seed and mince the jalapeño peppers.

2. Add the chopped onion, lime juice, minced fresh and pickled jalapeños and jalapeño juice to the shrimp. Toss to mix.

6 SERVINGS

CREOLE SHRIMP

These spicy shrimp keep guests coming back again and again, so I often double the recipe. Sprinkle some fresh chopped parsley on for color just before serving. You can buy Creole seasoning blend in supermarkets. It has a lot of flavor and just the right amount of kick. You could also use a blackened seafood seasoning blend; however, then you may want to use about half.

1 pound medium-large shelled and deveined shrimp
2 tablespoons Creole seasoning
2 tablespoons lemon juice
1 tablespoon honey
3 tablespoons olive oil

1. In a medium bowl, toss the shrimp with the Creole seasoning, lemon juice, honey and oil until the shrimp are well coated. Let stand for 5 minutes.

2. Heat a large heavy frying pan over high heat. Add the shrimp with its marinade and cook, stirring occasionally, until the shrimp are curled, about 3 minutes. Serve hot on toothpicks.

4 TO 6 SERVINGS

JALAPEÑO PEPPERS STUFFED WITH TUNA

Our friend John Lazaro is famous for stuffing jalapeño peppers with tuna salad. This adaptation of his recipe gets high praise every time we serve it. Be warned though: Even though the mayonnaise soothes the heat of the peppers, this appetizer is not for timid taste buds. Often jalapeño peppers are pickled with carrots. If so, use the carrots as a garnish.

12 whole pickled jalapeño peppers
1 can (6$\frac{1}{8}$ ounces) solid tuna packed in water
1 celery rib
1 tablespoon minced onion
3 tablespoons mayonnaise

1. Drain the jalapeño peppers. Cut each one in half lengthwise, then scrape out the seeds, rinse the peppers and pat dry. Arrange them, cut sides up, on a serving platter.

2. Drain the tuna. Place it in a small mixing bowl and flake with a fork. Finely chop the celery. Stir the chopped celery, minced onion and mayonnaise into the tuna. Fill each pepper half with about 1 teaspoon of the tuna mixture, depending on the size of the pepper.

MAKES 24

7 FROM THE GRILL

Grilling is synonymous with quick cooking. So while the tantalizing aroma of foods turning a succulent golden brown over hot coals stimulates appetites, specialty appetizers, such as Barbecued Oysters, Grilled Ratatouille, Grilled Scallops with Spicy Black Beans and Garlicky Pork Kebabs, will be ready to assuage that hunger in ten minutes or less.

Grilling provides instant entertainment as well, and for a 5 in 10 cook, the smoke serves as a sixth flavoring ingredient. Today, with the availability of instant-on gas-fired grills, people living in all climates can enjoy barbecued food throughout the year. However, if grilling isn't for you, the recipes in this chapter also can be prepared under the broiler.

A note about grilling: Of all the cooking methods, it's the most inexact. Since it's difficult to control the temperature, cooking times may vary as well. Always test for doneness before removing the food from the grill and serving it.

Remember, too, that if you are using wooden or bamboo skewers, they should be soaked for about 30 minutes before grilling so they don't char.

GRILLED GARLIC PITAS

You don't have to wait for the fire to be perfectly hot to grill pita toasts. These savory snacks help stave off hunger while guests are waiting for the rest of the meal.

1 package (10 ounces) mini pita breads
4 tablespoons butter
1 large garlic clove
2 teaspoons Italian herb seasoning
   Few drops of hot pepper sauce

1. Light a medium-hot fire on a barbecue grill or preheat the broiler.

2. Split each pita bread horizontally into 2 thin rounds. Melt the butter. Mince the garlic. Stir the garlic, herbs and hot sauce into the butter.

3. Grill or broil the bread 3 to 4 inches from the source of heat about 1 minute, just until the pita is heated through and begins to brown. Watch carefully that the pitas don't burn.

4. Brush each pita with the melted garlic butter and serve warm.

MAKES 24

FRESH GARLIC TOMATO BREAD

The success of this popular Spanish tapas depends on using prime ingredients. To dress up these toasts, drape a paper-thin slice of prosciutto or cured ham on top. This is a good appetizer to remember when you're grilling because it can be made while the coals are still heating up for the main course.

1 large, very ripe tomato
4 slices of country-style bread, cut about 1/2 inch thick
2 garlic cloves, split in half
2 tablespoons extra virgin olive oil

1. Preheat the broiler or grill. Cut the tomato in half and squeeze out most of the seeds. On the grill, toast the bread on one side, watching carefully to be sure it doesn't burn. Then rub each piece with half a clove of garlic.

2. Turn the bread over and toast the other side. Rub this side with garlic, too.

3. Rub the cut tomato into the bread. Then drizzle on the olive oil. Cut each slice of bread in half diagonally and serve while still warm.

4 SERVINGS

GRILLED EGGPLANT SANDWICHES

Grilling imparts a wonderful smoky flavor to eggplant. For this tasty appetizer, garlic Jack cheese is melted on top of grilled eggplant slices. They are delicious served on bruschetta—grilled Italian bread.

1 medium eggplant (about 1 pound)
¼ cup olive oil
1 tablespoon chopped fresh oregano or 1 teaspoon dried oregano
4 ounces of thinly sliced garlic Jack cheese
10 thin slices of Italian bread

1. Light a medium-hot fire in the barbecue grill. Trim the ends off the eggplant and cut crosswise into 10 rounds about ½ inch thick. Brush the eggplant slices lightly with about 1 tablespoon of the olive oil and place them oiled side down on the grill. Brush the tops with another tablespoon of olive oil and season with the oregano. Grill, turning occasionally and brushing with oil, until the eggplant is soft, about 8 minutes total cooking time. When the eggplant is almost done, top each piece with a small slice of cheese and continue grilling until the cheese melts, 1 to 2 minutes.

2. Meanwhile, grill the bread until golden brown on each side, about 1 minute per side, depending on the heat of the fire. Drizzle any remaining olive oil over the bread and top with an eggplant slice. Serve warm.

3 TO 4 SERVINGS

GRILLED RATATOUILLE

Once you've tried ratatouille cooked on a grill, you may not want it cooked any other way. If you have an herb garden, throw a generous handful of chopped fresh thyme, marjoram, oregano and basil into the salad when you toss it. Or use herbes de Provence.

1 pound eggplant (1 small) or Japanese eggplant
1 pound small zucchini (about 5)
¼ cup extra virgin olive oil
1 jar (15 ounces) roasted sweet red peppers
1 tablespoon herbes de Provence
Salt and pepper

1. Light a medium-hot fire in a barbecue grill. Cut the eggplant lengthwise into ½-inch-thick slices. Cut the zucchini lengthwise in half.

2. Brush the vegetables with olive oil and place over the hottest part of the fire. Grill, turning occasionally, 6 to 8 minutes, until the vegetables are tender and lightly browned. Drain the red peppers. Place them on the grill about 3 minutes, to heat through.

3. When the vegetables are done, cut them into bite-size pieces and toss them with the remaining olive oil and herbs. Season with salt and freshly ground pepper to taste.

6 TO 8 SERVINGS

GRILLED SUMMER SQUASH WITH MUSTARD GLAZE

For contrasting color, use both yellow and green pattypan squash. Thread the squash halves on long metal skewers so you don't have to turn them over one at a time.

16 small (1 1/2 inches in diameter) pattypan squash
  (about 1 pound)
 4 tablespoons butter
 2 teaspoons Dijon mustard
 2 teaspoons dried thyme leaves
 1/4 teaspoon salt
 1/4 teaspoon freshly ground pepper

1. Light a medium-hot fire in a barbecue grill or preheat the broiler. Rinse the squash and trim off the stems. Then cut each squash in half horizontally into 2 slices. Thread the squash slices onto metal skewers so that they lie flat.

2. In a small saucepan, melt the butter. Stir in the mustard, thyme, salt and pepper. Brush the mustard butter over the squash. Place the squash on the grill and brush the other side with the mustard butter. Grill 3 minutes. Turn the squash kebabs over and baste again with the butter sauce. Grill about 3 minutes longer, or until the squash is soft and nicely browned. (Or cook about 8 minutes in the broiler 3 to 4 inches from the heat, basting occasionally with the butter.)

MAKES 32

CILANTRO CHICKEN KEBABS

Season fruity olive oil with chopped garlic, fresh cilantro and ground cumin for a tasty baste for appetizer chicken kebabs. They're delicious cold as well as hot off the grill.

1 pound skinless, boneless chicken breasts
2 large garlic cloves
3 tablespoons extra virgin olive oil
2 tablespoons chopped fresh cilantro
1 teaspoon ground cumin

1. Light a medium-hot fire in the barbecue or preheat the broiler. Cut the chicken breasts lengthwise into ³/₄-inch-wide strips. Thread the chicken strips onto 12 metal or soaked bamboo skewers.

2. Mince the garlic. In a small bowl, combine the garlic, oil, cilantro and cumin. Brush some of the garlic oil over the chicken strips.

3. Grill or broil 3 to 4 inches from the heat for 4 minutes. Baste the chicken with any remaining marinade, turn the skewers over and cook until the chicken is nicely browned on the outside and white to the center, 3 to 4 minutes longer.

MAKES 12

CHICKEN SATAY

These chicken skewers are served with a great Indonesian-inspired peanut sauce.

    1 pound skinless, boneless chicken breasts
    ¹/₂ teaspoon salt
    ¹/₄ teaspoon freshly ground pepper
    2 medium garlic cloves
    ¹/₃ cup extra chunky peanut butter
    2 tablespoons soy sauce
 1¹/₂ teaspoons grated fresh ginger

1. Preheat the broiler. Cut the chicken breasts lengthwise into strips about ³/₄ inch wide. Thread the chicken onto 12 metal or soaked bamboo skewers. Season with the salt and pepper.

2. Crush the garlic through a press into a small bowl. Blend in the peanut butter, soy sauce, ginger and ¹/₄ cup hot water to make a spreadable sauce. If necessary, add a little more water.

3. Arrange the chicken skewers on a broiler pan. Broil 3 to 4 inches from the heat for 3 minutes. Turn over, brush with the sauce and continue broiling until the chicken is done, about 3 minutes longer. Serve with the remaining sauce for dipping.

MAKES 12

SESAME CHICKEN STRIPS

Chinese hoisin sauce makes a terrific basting sauce for grilled chicken. You can find it in Asian markets and many supermarkets. Keep a careful eye on these kebabs as they cook.

1 pound skinless, boneless chicken breasts
3 tablespoons bottled hoisin sauce
1 tablespoon cider vinegar
1 teaspoon chopped garlic
1¹/₂ teaspoons sesame seeds

1. Light a medium-hot fire in the barbecue grill or preheat the broiler. Cut the chicken lengthwise into ³/₄-inch-wide strips. Thread the chicken strips onto small metal or soaked bamboo skewers.

2. Combine the hoisin sauce, vinegar and garlic. Brush the sauce over the chicken. Then sprinkle on the sesame seeds, pressing them into the sauce.

3. Grill or broil 3 to 4 inches from the heat for 3 minutes. Turn the chicken over and grill about 3 minutes longer, until the chicken is white throughout but still moist in the center. Serve hot.

MAKES ABOUT 12

TROPICAL CHICKEN KEBABS

Cubes of chicken and pineapple are basted with a lemony curry butter and then cooked over a grill until succulent and golden brown.

2 pounds skinless, boneless chicken breasts
1 can (20 ounces) pineapple chunks in their own juice
4 tablespoons butter
2 lemons
1 teaspoon curry powder

1. Light a medium-hot fire in a barbecue grill or preheat the broiler. Cut the chicken into 1-inch cubes. You'll have around 40. Drain the pineapple, reserving the juice. Thread the chicken and pineapple chunks alternately on skewers, allowing approximately 2 of each per skewer.

2. In a small saucepan, melt the butter. Squeeze the juice from half of 1 lemon into the butter and add the curry powder and 2 tablespoons of the reserved pineapple juice.

3. Grill the chicken skewers, basting frequently with the butter and turning occasionally, about 6 to 8 minutes total cooking time, until the chicken is golden brown outside and white in the center but still moist. Or broil 3 to 4 inches from the source of heat for about 6 minutes. Meanwhile, cut the remaining lemons into wedges and serve alongside.

MAKES ABOUT 20

CHICKEN SAUSAGE AND APPLE KEBABS

Everyone loves sausages, especially when they are grilled and served with a creamy-sweet mustard dipping sauce. One timesaving tip is to use an apple corer/slicer to core the apple and divide it into wedges in one quick motion.

1 pound chicken sausages
3 tart apples
1 tablespoon vegetable oil
$1/4$ cup hot-sweet mustard, preferably Russian style
$1/4$ cup heavy cream

1. Light a medium-hot fire in the barbecue grill or preheat the broiler. Cut the sausages into $1\frac{1}{2}$-inch lengths. Core the apples and cut each one into 8 wedges. Thread 3 pieces of sausage and 2 apple wedges on each of 12 metal or soaked bamboo skewers.

2. Lightly brush the kebabs with oil and grill or broil 3 to 4 inches from the heat, turning occasionally, about 8 minutes, until the sausages are browned outside and cooked through.

3. Combine the mustard and cream, blending well. Serve the mustard sauce with the kebabs.

MAKES 12

APPETIZER BEEF SKEWERS WITH STROGANOFF SAUCE

Prepared vinaigrette or Italian salad dressing makes an instant marinade for beef kebabs. Grill them over hot coals on an instant-on gas grill or cook them quickly under the broiler.

1 pound boneless sirloin steak, cut 1 inch thick
2 tablespoons vinaigrette or Italian salad dressing
$1/2$ teaspoon salt
$1/4$ teaspoon freshly ground pepper
$1/2$ cup sour cream or nonfat plain yogurt
1 tablespoon drained prepared white horseradish
1 teaspoon Worcestershire sauce

1. Light a medium-hot fire in a barbecue grill or preheat the broiler. Cut the steak into 1-inch cubes and place the beef cubes in a bowl. Pour in the vinaigrette and stir until the beef is well coated with the marinade.

2. Thread 4 or 5 pieces of steak on 6-inch presoaked wooden or small metal skewers. Season with the salt and pepper. Grill or broil 3 to 4 inches from the heat, turning once, about 5 minutes, or until the steak reaches desired doneness.

3. In a small bowl, stir together the sour cream, horseradish and Worcestershire sauce until well blended. Slide the steak cubes off their skewers and serve with toothpicks, with the dipping sauce on the side.

MAKES ABOUT 18

GARLICKY PORK KEBABS

Cook these savory appetizer kebabs quickly on an instant-on gas-fired grill or under the broiler.

$1/2$ pound boneless pork loin
$1/2$ pound small zucchini (about 3)
 2 tablespoons extra virgin olive oil
 2 teaspoons bottled minced garlic in oil
 2 teaspoons chopped fresh rosemary
$1/2$ teaspoon salt
$1/4$ teaspoon freshly ground pepper

1. Light a medium-hot fire in a barbecue grill or preheat the broiler. Cut the pork into 1-inch cubes. Trim the ends from the zucchini and cut them crosswise into $3/4$-inch rounds. In a medium bowl, combine the pork, zucchini, olive oil, garlic, rosemary, salt and pepper. Toss to mix evenly.

2. Thread the pork and zucchini on small skewers, using 2 pork cubes and 2 zucchini slices for each skewer.

3. Grill or broil 3 to 4 inches from the heat for about 6 minutes, or until the pork is nicely browned on the outside and cooked through. Serve hot.

MAKES ABOUT 18

GRILLED FIGS WRAPPED IN PROSCIUTTO

12 ripe fresh figs
12 thin slices prosciutto
2 tablespoons vegetable oil
1/2 cup plain yogurt
2 tablespoons chopped mint

1. Light a medium-hot fire in a barbecue grill. Wrap each fig with a slice of prosciutto.

2. When the fire is ready, clean the grill with a wire brush. Then oil the grill to prevent sticking. Place the figs on the grill and cook, turning once, until heated through, about 5 minutes.

3. In a small bowl, blend the yogurt and mint. Serve the grilled figs hot, with a dollop of minted yogurt on the side.

MAKES 12

BARBECUED OYSTERS

Oysters are one of the best things you can produce on a barbecue grill. They even tell you when they're done. As soon as they open, they're ready to eat. When you place the oysters on the grill, check that the rounded side is down so that none of the flavorful liquor will drain out. The recipe for a tangy dipping sauce is included, although you may find that you prefer barbecued oysters without any additional embellishment.

24 large oysters in the shell
$^1/_2$ cup white wine vinegar
 1 tablespoon finely chopped parsley
 1 teaspoon chopped garlic
 Few drops of hot pepper sauce

1. Light a hot fire in a barbecue grill. When the coals are white hot, arrange the oysters on the grill with the rounded side down. As soon as the oyster shells pop open, remove them with a large spoon to a serving platter. Discard any oysters that don't open. Cooking time will be about 5 minutes, although it will vary depending on the size of the oysters and how cold they are. You can also roast them in a preheated 475 degree F. oven for about 8 minutes.

2. Combine the vinegar, parsley, garlic and hot pepper sauce and serve with the oysters.

MAKES 24

GRILLED SALMON WITH LIME CHILI BUTTER

Grilling works magic for salmon. Whenever you grill fish, be sure to clean the grill with a wire brush and oil it, if necessary, to prevent sticking.

1 pound salmon fillets (about ³/₄ inch thick)
4 tablespoons butter
    Grated zest of 1 lime
2 tablespoons tequila
¹/₂ teaspoon chili powder

1. Light a medium-hot fire in a barbecue grill or preheat the broiler. Cut the salmon into 1-inch cubes. Thread the salmon cubes onto 4 small metal or soaked wooden skewers.

2. Grill or broil 3 to 4 inches from the heat for about 7 minutes, until the salmon is cooked through but still moist.

3. While the salmon is grilling, melt the butter in a small saucepan. Remove from the heat and stir in the lime zest, tequila and chili powder. Serve the salmon as soon as it comes off the grill with the chili butter sauce for dipping.

4 SERVINGS

BROILED SCALLOPS WITH NEW POTATOES AND TARRAGON CREAM

This is a light, elegant starter. For extra color, place a spinach leaf or other dark green leaf under each portion.

8 small new potatoes (about 1½-inch diameter, 10 ounces)
8 large sea scallops (about ½ pound)
¼ teaspoon salt
¼ teaspoon freshly ground pepper
⅓ cup mayonnaise
2 tablespoons tarragon white wine vinegar plus 1 teaspoon chopped tarragon leaves (from the vinegar)
1 ounce salmon roe or golden caviar (whitefish roe)

1. Preheat the broiler. Arrange the potatoes in a ring in a microwave-safe baking dish. Add 1 tablespoon of water and cover with plastic wrap. Microwave on High for about 5 minutes, until the potatoes are tender. Let stand 2 minutes.

2. Meanwhile, cut each scallop into thirds. Arrange the slices on a baking sheet and season with salt and pepper. Broil 3 to 4 inches from the heat about 2 minutes, until done, being careful not to overcook.

3. Combine the mayonnaise, tarragon vinegar and leaves.

4. To serve: Cut each potato into 3 slices. On each of 8 appetizer plates, alternate slices of potatoes and scallops in a row. Spoon a ribbon of tarragon mayonnaise partially over the potatoes and scallops. Garnish with the salmon roe.

8 SERVINGS

GRILLED SCALLOPS WITH SPICY BLACK BEANS

Sweet succulent scallops turn to smoky perfection cooked over a grill. They make an excellent first course served over savory black beans.

1 pound sea scallops
2 bunches of green onions (about 6 each)
1 can (15 ounces) black beans
1/2 cup thick and chunky medium-hot tomato salsa
2 tablespoons olive oil

1. Light a medium-hot fire in a barbecue grill or preheat the broiler. If the scallops are large, cut them in half; you want 24 pieces. Thread the scallops on long metal or soaked bamboo skewers. Trim the root end off the green onions. Rinse and drain the black beans and place them in a microwave-safe bowl. Stir in the salsa. Cover tightly with microwave-safe plastic wrap. Microwave on High for 3 to 4 minutes, until heated through.

2. When the fire is ready, clean the grill with a wire brush and oil it, if necessary, to prevent sticking. Grill or broil the scallops and green onions 3 to 4 inches from the heat, turning once and brushing occasionally with olive oil, for about 4 minutes, until the scallops are nicely browned and opaque throughout and the green onions are lightly browned and softened. Remove the scallops from the skewers and serve them on the warm beans. Garnish each serving with grilled green onions.

4 SERVINGS

TERIYAKI SHRIMP

Grilling shrimp with their shells on keeps them moister. These spicy shrimp are good served hot off the grill or at room temperature.

1 pound medium-large shrimp
$\frac{1}{3}$ cup bottled teriyaki sauce
2 tablespoons rice wine or dry sherry
1 tablespoon grated fresh ginger
1 teaspoon sesame chili oil

1. Light a hot fire in a barbecue grill or preheat the broiler. Rinse the shrimp under cold water and pat dry. Combine the teriyaki sauce, rice wine, ginger and sesame chili oil in a medium bowl. Add the shrimp and stir to mix well. Let stand 5 minutes.

2. Thread 3 to 4 shrimp each onto oiled metal or soaked bamboo skewers. Grill or broil 3 to 4 inches from the heat about 2 minutes per side, until the shrimp turn bright pink. If you like, bring the basting sauce to a boil and boil 1 minute. Serve as a dip for the shrimp.

4 TO 6 SERVINGS

SWORDFISH BROCHETTES WITH MANGO LIME SAUCE

1 pound swordfish steak, cut about ³/₄ inch thick
16 to 18 cherry tomatoes
1 lime
¹/₃ cup mango nectar
²/₃ cup mayonnaise

1. Light a medium-hot fire in a barbecue grill or preheat the broiler. Cut the swordfish into ³/₄-inch cubes. Thread the fish cubes and cherry tomatoes near the tips of 16 to 18 soaked short wooden skewers.

2. Use a coarse grater to remove the zest from the lime. Then squeeze the juice from the lime. Combine 1¹/₂ tablespoons lime juice and 1¹/₂ tablespoons mango nectar and baste the kebabs. Grill or broil 3 to 4 inches from the heat, turning for 5 to 7 minutes, until the fish is lightly browned but still juicy.

3. In a small bowl, blend the remaining mango nectar with the lime zest and mayonnaise. Serve as a dipping sauce with the brochettes.

MAKES 16 TO 18

GRILLED TUNA AND ENDIVE SALAD

Grilling imparts an appealing smoky flavor to this first-course tuna salad that combines the grilled fish with bittersweet endive, green onions and cubes of warm, ripe tomatoes. You may want to garnish this salad with olives.

1 bunch of green onions (about 6)
2 heads of Belgian endive
1 large ripe tomato
1 pound fresh tuna fillet
¼ cup olive oil vinaigrette salad dressing
   Salt and pepper

1. Light a medium-hot fire in a barbecue grill. Trim the root end off the green onions and cut off half of the green leaves. Cut each endive lengthwise in half. Cut the tomato in half.

2. Lightly brush the tuna, green onions, endive and tomato with the vinaigrette. Place them on the grill and cook, turning, until the tuna is just cooked through and the vegetables are tender and lightly browned. Depending on the temperature of your fire, the tomato and green onions will take about 3 minutes, the endive about 4 minutes and the tuna about 6 minutes. When the ingredients are done, remove them from the grill and cut into 1-inch dice. Place everything in a medium bowl and toss gently with the remaining vinaigrette. Serve warm or at room temperature.

4 SERVINGS

TUNA KEBABS WITH WASABI BUTTER

Wasabi, Japanese horseradish, is a great convenience. Keep the pale green powder in your pantry to dissolve in water any time you want to add sharp, pungent flavor to a sauce. Wasabi is sold in Asian and specialty markets and in many supermarkets. Be sure to clean the grill with a wire brush and to oil it, if necessary, to prevent the fish from sticking.

2 pounds fresh tuna fillets, preferably ahi
3 tablespoons vegetable oil
1/4 teaspoon salt
1/4 teaspoon freshly ground pepper
1 stick (1/2 cup) butter
1 tablespoon wasabi

1. Light a medium-hot fire in a barbecue grill or preheat the broiler. Cut the tuna into 1-inch cubes. Thread the fish on long metal skewers for easy turning. Brush with the oil and season with the salt and pepper.

2. Grill or broil the fish 3 to 4 inches from heat, turning once, for about 7 minutes, until cooked through but still moist.

3. Meanwhile, melt the butter in a small saucepan. Dissolve the wasabi in 1 tablespoon water and stir into the melted butter. Remove the tuna cubes from the skewers and place them on a platter. Serve with toothpicks, with the wasabi butter for dipping.

8 SERVINGS

8 Salads and Other Cool First Courses

According to etymologists, the word *salad* comes from the Latin word *sal,* meaning something salted. The idea probably originated with people dipping wild greens into salt.

With today's emphasis on lighter eating and the availability of superb produce, delicious salads can include almost any ingredient imaginable, as long as the various components complement each other in taste, texture, size and color.

Although you can buy many salad greens already cleaned, here's a quick preparation technique that professional cooks use. Fill the sink or large deep bowl with cold water. Add the salad greens and gently swish them around, allowing any sand to sink to the bottom. Then carefully lift the leaves out of the water, transfer them to a salad spinner and spin dry.

The wide-ranging collection of refreshing first-course salads in this chapter includes: Arugula with Pears and Stilton, Smoked Trout with Spinach, Red Onions and Orange Vinaigrette, Papaya and Avocado with Bay Shrimp, and Tuna with White Beans and Tapenade.

This chapter also includes a couple of cold soups, which can be ladled into bowls as a cool first course, or served in glass punch cups as an appetizer.

TWO BEAN SALAD

Fresh green beans and canned white beans pair in this appetizer salad. You could also add cubes of smoked chicken or cooked shelled baby shrimp. It's best to dress this salad just before you serve it to preserve the bright color of the green beans.

3/4 pound fresh green beans
1 can (15 ounces) white cannellini beans
1/2 cup minced red onion
1/3 cup bottled olive oil and vinegar dressing
1 teaspoon dried thyme leaves

1. In a pot of boiling salted water, cook the green beans until just tender, about 5 minutes. Drain and rinse under cold running water; drain well.

2. Rinse and drain the canned white beans and add them to the green beans along with the minced onion. Pour the dressing over the salad. Add the thyme and toss gently to coat the vegetables with the dressing.

4 TO 6 SERVINGS

CORN SALAD WITH BASIL AND TOMATOES

Sweet corn kernels are tossed with corn salad, otherwise known as mâche or lamb's lettuce, ripe cherry tomatoes and fresh basil in this colorful first-course salad. Although the nutty-flavored mâche is considered a gourmet green, it grows wild throughout the country, and is easy to grow in backyard gardens. If you have trouble finding it, however, substitute any small-leafed lettuce or mixture of greens.

6 cups mâche or butter lettuce
1 pint small ripe cherry tomatoes
½ cup tightly packed basil leaves
1 cup sweet corn kernels (fresh or thawed frozen)
½ cup bottled Italian vinaigrette dressing with Parmesan cheese

1. Rinse the mâche and spin dry. Rinse and dry the tomatoes. Rinse the basil, pat dry and cut it into thin shreds.

2. Place the mâche, tomatoes, basil and corn in a salad bowl. Pour on the dressing and toss until all of the ingredients are well coated. Serve immediately.

4 SERVINGS

EGGPLANT PUREE ON WATERCRESS

For a dramatic presentation, mound the garlicky eggplant spread on a bed of watercress leaves and poke a few triangles of thinly sliced, toasted country-style bread into the top of the dip. Serve more toast on the side.

1 medium eggplant (about 1 pound)
3 tablespoons extra virgin olive oil
1 teaspoon chopped garlic
1 bunch of watercress (about 5 ounces)
1½ tablespoons nonfat plain yogurt
½ teaspoon salt

1. Peel the eggplant and cut it crosswise into ¾-inch-thick slices. Heat a large frying pan over high heat. Add half of the oil, the garlic and as many eggplant slices as you can fit in one layer. Cook the eggplant over medium-high heat until tender and golden brown on both sides, about 3 minutes. Remove the eggplant to a cutting board. Cook the rest of the eggplant in the remaining oil.

2. Cut off the thick stems of the watercress and discard. Rinse the watercress leaves and spin dry. Arrange the watercress on a large platter or 6 individual plates.

3. When all the eggplant is cooked, finely chop it with a sharp chef's knife. Place the eggplant in a bowl. Stir in the yogurt and salt. Spoon the eggplant over the watercress and serve.

6 SERVINGS

GREEN ONIONS NICOISE

Use your best olive oil for this recipe. It will make all the difference. Braised young leeks are also delicious topped with this warm olive, tomato and basil relish.

4 bunches of green onions
1 medium tomato
3 tablespoons extra virgin olive oil
1 cup tightly packed fresh basil leaves
3 ounces oil-cured black olives (about 1/2 cup)

1. Pour 1 inch of water in a large frying pan and bring it to a boil over high heat. Trim away the root ends of the green onions and enough of the green leaves so that the onions are 5 inches long. Rinse them. When the water comes to a boil, add 1 teaspoon salt and the onions. Simmer until the onions are tender, about 3 minutes. Then drain and arrange them on a platter.

2. While the green onions are cooking, cut the tomato into 3/4-inch dice.

3. Dry the frying pan, then pour in the olive oil and heat over high heat for 30 seconds. Stir in the tomato, basil and olives. Cook, stirring frequently, until the tomato begins to soften, 2 to 3 minutes. Pour the tomato relish over the green onions and serve warm.

6 SERVINGS

MUSHROOM AND PARMESAN SALAD

The top of this salad is garnished with curls of Parmesan cheese. Be sure to use authentic Parmigiano-Reggiano from Italy for the best flavor—there are plenty of imported "Parmesan" cheeses out there, but search out the real thing, which has its name stamped on the rind. You won't be using the whole chunk of cheese, but select a large piece with a flat side for ease in shaving the curls.

1 pound large mushrooms
2 celery ribs
3 tablespoons fresh lemon juice
$1/4$ teaspoon salt
$1/4$ teaspoon freshly ground pepper
$2/3$ cup olive oil
6 ounces imported Parmesan cheese, in 1 piece

1. Thinly slice the mushrooms and the celery. Toss them together in a large bowl.

2. In a small bowl, whisk the lemon juice, salt and pepper. Gradually whisk in the oil until well blended. Pour over the mushrooms and celery and mix well.

3. Divide the salad among 4 to 6 salad plates. Using a swivel-bladed vegetable peeler or a cheese planer, shave curls of cheese from the flat side of the chunk of cheese, pressing hard on the peeler, and letting the curls fall over the top of the salad. You will probably not use the entire chunk of cheese; about 8 large curls for each salad is enough. Serve immediately.

4 TO 6 SERVINGS

RADISHES AND RED ONION SALAD

Guests always come back for seconds after they taste this unusual salad. I like to serve this colorful combination family-style on a platter bordered with endive spears or small leaves of romaine lettuce with which to eat it. To save time, use your food processor to slice the onion and radishes.

1 small red onion
2 bunches of red radishes
1 can (15 ounces) mandarin orange segments
2 tablespoons extra virgin olive oil
1 tablespoon red wine vinegar

1. Halve and thinly slice the red onion. Rinse the radishes and thinly slice them. Drain the orange segments, reserving 2 tablespoons of the syrup.

2. In a bowl, gently toss the sliced onions, radishes and oranges together with the olive oil and vinegar. Add the reserved orange syrup and toss again. Pour the salad onto a deep platter and serve at room temperature.

4 TO 6 SERVINGS

SPINACH SALAD WITH KALAMATA OLIVES, TOMATOES AND FETA

1 bag (10 ounces) ready-to-use spinach leaves
1 pint ripe cherry tomatoes
½ cup homemade or bottled red wine oil and vinegar dressing
1 package (4 ounces) crumbled feta cheese
1 cup pitted Kalamata olives

1. Place the spinach in a salad bowl. Rinse the cherry tomatoes, cut them in half and add them to the salad bowl.

2. Pour the dressing over the spinach and toss gently to coat the spinach and tomatoes.

3. Sprinkle the feta and olives over the salad and serve.

4 TO 6 SERVINGS

FRESH MOZZARELLA TOMATO SALAD

Remember this lovely first-course salad when tomatoes are perfectly ripe. Although basil is a favorite herb with tomatoes and soft, delicately flavored fresh mozzarella, you could also use fresh marjoram, oregano or lemon thyme.

1 pound fresh mozzarella (2 balls)
2 ripe beefsteak tomatoes
1 red onion
1 cup loosely packed fresh basil leaves
1/3 cup extra virgin olive oil
   Salt and freshly ground pepper

1. Cut each ball of mozzarella into 6 slices. Cut each tomato into 6 slices. Thinly slice the red onions and separate them into rings.

2. Shred the basil leaves.

3. Alternate slices of tomato and mozzarella on a serving platter. Scatter the onion rings and basil over them. Drizzle the olive oil over the salad. Season with salt and pepper to taste and serve.

4 TO 6 SERVINGS

WATERCRESS AND TOMATO SALAD

When tomatoes are at the peak of ripeness, my husband, Edward, makes this light, refreshing first-course salad.

2 large ripe tomatoes
2 bunches of watercress (about 5 ounces each)
1/3 cup extra virgin olive oil
1 1/2 tablespoons red wine vinegar
1/4 teaspoon dry mustard
Salt and freshly ground pepper

1. Bring a small saucepan of water to a boil. Cut a small "X" in the bottom of each tomato and remove the stem at the opposite end. Place the tomatoes in the boiling water for about 30 seconds. Then drain and place them under cold, running water. When the tomatoes are cool enough to handle, slip off the peels. Cut each tomato in half and gently squeeze out the seeds. Coarsely chop the tomatoes.

2. Rinse the watercress and spin dry. In a large bowl, whisk together the olive oil, vinegar and dry mustard. Season to taste with salt and pepper. Add the watercress and toss gently until it's well coated with the dressing. Then gently fold in the tomatoes. Divide the salad among 6 plates and serve.

6 SERVINGS

FENNEL AND APPLE SALAD

Red-skinned apples add a spot of bright color to this crisp fennel salad. Use an apple corer/slicer to save time removing the core and separating the apples into wedges. You may also want to toast the pecans, about 5 minutes in a 375 degree F. oven, to intensify their nutty fragrance and flavor.

1 large bulb of fresh fennel (about ³/₄ pound)
2 medium red-skinned apples
¹/₃ cup prepared chunky blue cheese salad dressing
1¹/₂ tablespoons red wine vinegar
¹/₄ cup pecan pieces

1. Trim the stems, root end and any tough outer leaves from the fennel. Slice it in half lengthwise. Then place the halves, cut sides down, on a cutting board and thinly slice.

2. Core the apples and cut them into thin wedges. On 4 individual salad plates, arrange overlapping slices of fennel and apples in a sunburst pattern.

3. Thin the salad dressing with the vinegar. Then spoon or drizzle the dressing over the fennel and apples. Sprinkle on the pecans and serve.

4 SERVINGS

ARUGULA WITH PEARS AND STILTON

Peppery arugula, sweet juicy pears and rich, zesty Stilton star in this sophisticated first-course salad.

3 bunches of arugula (about 1/2 pound)
1/3 cup extra virgin olive oil
1 1/2 tablespoons balsamic vinegar
1/2 teaspoon salt
1/4 teaspoon freshly ground pepper
2 ripe pears
1/4 pound Stilton cheese

1. Rinse the arugula and spin dry. Pour the olive oil into a salad bowl. Whisk in the vinegar. Season with the salt and freshly ground pepper. Place the arugula in the salad bowl over the dressing.

2. Cut the pears in half and use a melon baller or small spoon to core them. Then slice the pears into thin wedges and add to the salad bowl. Crumble the Stilton over the pears and gently toss the ingredients together.

3. Divide the salad into 4 portions and serve.

4 SERVINGS

SWISS SALAD

Cubes of nutty-flavored Swiss cheese, sweet beets and crisp tart apples are combined in this colorful, tasty appetizer salad. If you like, you could also toss in some walnut pieces.

1/2 pound Swiss cheese
1 can (16 ounces) sliced beets
1 tart green apple
2 tablespoons extra virgin olive oil
2 tablespoons red wine vinegar
1/4 teaspoon salt
1/4 teaspoon freshly ground pepper

1. Cut the cheese into 1/2-inch cubes. Drain the beets and cut them into 1/2-inch pieces. Core the apple and cut into 1/2-inch cubes.

2. In a serving bowl, whisk together the olive oil, vinegar, salt and pepper. Add the cheese, beets and apple. Toss gently to coat well and serve.

6 SERVINGS

CHINESE SESAME NOODLES

Quick-cooking Chinese-style chow mein noodles are available in the refrigerated case of well-stocked supermarkets. You can embellish this quick first-course salad with shredded cooked chicken, sliced radishes, diced cucumber, whatever you happen to have on hand.

1 package (12 ounces) fresh Chinese-style chow mein
    noodles or vermicelli
1 bunch of green onions
⅓ cup tahini
3 tablespoons bottled teriyaki sauce
2 teaspoons bottled chopped garlic in oil
½ teaspoon salt
    Freshly ground pepper

1. In a large pot of boiling salted water, cook the noodles according to package directions until tender but still firm, 2 to 3 minutes. Drain, reserving about ⅓ cup of the cooking water.

2. While the noodles are cooking, thinly slice the green onions, including most of the green part.

3. Add the warm cooking water to the tahini and stir until smooth. Add the green onions, teriyaki sauce, garlic, salt and pepper. Blend well, then pour over the noodles and toss gently until the noodles are well coated with the sauce. Serve immediately or refrigerate and serve cold.

4 TO 6 SERVINGS

SMOKED TURKEY AND JICAMA WITH PESTO MAYONNAISE AND PINEAPPLE

Nowadays in supermarkets you can buy a whole fresh pineapple that's peeled and ready to use. Top slices of the juicy sweet pineapple with a refreshing mixture of shredded smoked turkey and strips of crunchy jicama lightly dressed with pesto mayonnaise.

1/2 pound sliced smoked turkey breast
1 small jicama
1/3 cup mayonnaise
3 tablespoons prepared basil pesto
6 slices (about 1/2 inch thick) fresh or canned pineapple

1. Stack the turkey slices on a cutting board and cut them diagonally into 3/4-inch-thick strips. Peel the jicama and cut it into 1/4- to 1/2-inch-thick slices. Then cut the slices into 1/4-inch-thick strips.

2. In a medium bowl, stir together the mayonnaise and pesto until blended. Add the turkey and jicama strips and toss to coat evenly.

3. Arrange the pineapple slices on 6 plates. Top with the smoked turkey salad. Serve immediately.

6 SERVINGS

PAPAYA AND AVOCADO
WITH BAY SHRIMP

This pretty first course combines wedges of buttery, pale green avocado with the sweet tropical flavors of vivid orange papaya, refreshing lime and delicate pale pink baby shrimp. If papayas aren't available, use peaches, nectarines or mangoes.

1 large ripe avocado
1 large ripe papaya
½ pound cooked shelled baby shrimp or cut-up larger shrimp
1 lime
3 tablespoons extra virgin olive oil

1. Cut the avocado in half and twist the halves to separate them. With a spoon, remove the pit. Then peel the avocado and cut each half lengthwise into 6 wedges. Cut the papaya in half and scoop out the seeds. Peel the papaya and cut each half lengthwise into 6 wedges.

2. Fan out 3 avocado wedges alternately with 3 papaya wedges on each of 4 individual salad plates. Rinse the shrimp and drain. Place a mound of shrimp on each plate where the wedges come together.

3. Remove the outermost colored part of the lime peel with a zester or swivel-bladed vegetable peeler. If using a peeler, finely chop the zest. Then juice half of the lime. Whisk together the lime juice and zest with the olive oil and drizzle the dressing over the fruit and shrimp.

4 SERVINGS

SMOKED TROUT WITH SPINACH, RED ONIONS AND ORANGE VINAIGRETTE

2 smoked trout (about 7 ounces each)
1 small red onion
2 navel oranges
1/3 cup extra virgin olive oil
    Salt and pepper
1 bag (10 ounces) ready-to-use spinach leaves

1. With a small paring knife, peel the skin from the smoked trout and lift off the fillets, discarding the bones.

2. Cut the onion into 1/4-inch slices. Separate them into rings. Using a sharp paring knife, trim both ends off the oranges just to the pulp. Then place the oranges on a board and cut away the peel and pith following the contour of the fruit. Holding the oranges over a large bowl to catch any juice, remove the sections by sliding your knife in and out along the membranes. Squeeze the membranes to extract any remaining juice.

3. Whisk the olive oil into the orange juice in the bowl. Season to taste with salt and freshly ground pepper. Add the spinach leaves and toss. Divide the spinach among 6 plates. Arrange the trout, orange sections and onion rings on top and serve.

6 SERVINGS

TUNA WITH WHITE BEANS AND TAPENADE

Feathery leaves of anise-flavored chervil season this flavorful mélange of tuna, white beans and black olive paste. Chervil grows like a weed if you have an herb garden or room in a planter box. It's also becoming more readily available in produce markets. If you can't locate fresh chervil, substitute about 1/3 cup of coarsely chopped fresh fennel leaves, flat leaf parsley or cilantro. I like to serve this savory mixture as an appetizer on thin slices of country-style bread, with endive spears or pieces of red cabbage, or as a first-course salad in radicchio or butter lettuce cups.

   1 can (12 1/4 ounces) solid white tuna packed in water
   1 can (15 ounces) small white beans
 1/3 cup coarsely chopped fresh chervil
   3 tablespoons tapenade (black olive paste)
   2 tablespoons extra virgin olive oil

1. Pour off most of the water from the tuna, place it in a medium bowl and flake slightly.

2. Rinse and drain the white beans. Add to the tuna.

3. Gently fold the chervil and tapenade into the tuna and white beans and pour into a serving dish. Drizzle the olive oil on top and serve.

4 TO 6 SERVINGS

VERY FINE VICHYSSOISE

Homemade cold potato and leek soup in 10 minutes? It's true. The trick is in using ice cubes in place of some of the liquid. Thanks to this recipe, I've become fonder of my microwave oven.

1 large russet potato (^{1}/$_2$ pound)
1 medium-size leek (^{1}/$_4$ pound)
1 can (10^1/$_2$ ounces) double-strength chicken broth
1 cup heavy cream or half-and-half
3 tablespoons chopped chives

1. Peel the potato and cut it into ^{1}/$_2$-inch slices. Place the potato slices in a single layer in a shallow microwave baking dish.

2. Trim the leek so that you are only using the white and pale green parts. Halve the leek lengthwise and cut crosswise into thin slices. Place the leek slices in a strainer and rinse well to remove any sand. Arrange the leeks over the potatoes. Add 2 tablespoons of water and cover tightly with microwave-safe plastic wrap. Microwave on High for 5 minutes. Remove and let stand 2 minutes.

3. Pour the leeks, potatoes and chicken broth into a blender and process 30 seconds. Then add 6 ice cubes and process another minute or so, until the ice cubes melt. Add the cream and process 10 seconds. Pour into glasses and garnish with chives.

6 SERVINGS

WHITE GAZPACHO

Serve this refreshing, spoonable salad in cocktail glasses.

2 celery ribs
1 medium cucumber (about 12 ounces)
1 can (14^1/$_2$ ounces) vegetable or chicken broth
^{1}/$_2$ cup diced green bell pepper
^{1}/$_2$ cup diced tomato

1. String the celery by breaking each rib near the bottom and pulling the strings down. Cut the celery into 2-inch lengths and place it in the blender.

2. Peel the cucumber, cut it in half lengthwise and scoop out the seeds with a small spoon or melon baller. Cut half of the cucumber into 2-inch lengths and place them in the blender. Cut the other half into ^{3}/$_4$-inch dice and reserve.

3. Pour the broth into the blender and process for about 2 minutes, until the mixture is smooth. Pour the gazpacho into glasses and garnish each serving with diced cucumber, green pepper and tomato.

4 TO 6 SERVINGS

INDEX